Cultural China

蘇州園林

The Classical Gardens of Suzhou

Li Zongwei

Better Link Press

This book is edited and designed by the Editorial Committee of *Cultural China* series

Managing Editors: Xu Naiqing, Wang Youbu, Wu Ying

Editors: Mina Choi, Yang Xinci

Text by Li Zongwei

Translation by Wang Houping and Cui Yingying (with Shanghai FESCO International Training Center)

Interior and Cover Design: Yuan Yinchang, Li Jing

ISBN-13: 978-1-60220-301-3

ISBN-10: 1-60220-301-6

Address any comments about *Travel through the Middle Kingdom: The Classical Gardens of Suzhou* to:

Better Link Press

99 Park Ave

New York, NY 10016

USA

or

Shanghai Press and Publishing Development Company

F 7 Donghu Road, Shanghai, China (200031)

Email: comments_betterlinkpress@hotmail.com

Computer typeset by Yuan Yinchang Design Studio, Shanghai

Printed in China by Shanghai Donnelley Printing Co. Ltd.

1   2   3   4   5   6   7   8   9   10

CONTENTS

Foreword

China, "*Zhong Guo*" as it is called in Mandarin Chinese, literally means "Middle Kingdom". This term originates from the 10th Century B.C. when the Zhou Dynasty was busy defending itself from encroaching barbarians. The Middle Kingdom then stretched from modern day Jiangsu in the east to Sichuan in the west, from Hebei in the north-east, and even encompassing parts of Gansu in the north-west. The Middle Kingdom was not a nation-state, but a celebration of a unified, highly-developed "central" culture. Cultural relics and artifacts, as well historical documents from this period, demonstrate how technologically advanced the Middle Kingdom was. From the creation of its uniquely sophisticated script to its metallurgical discoveries, and to the superb artistry of its craftsmen, the Middle Kingdom had no rivals in the East. Silk, magnificent bronzes and jades, and its complicated script all attest to the fact that the Kingdom was indeed the center of civilization in the East. It maintained its cultural supremacy for thousands of years, its influence encompassing Japan and Korea, and rippling all the way to Vietnam and Indonesia.

The term "Middle Kingdom" has since come to represent one of the oldest civilizations in the world. The Great Wall of China, the Terracotta Warriors of Xi'an, the Forbidden City, just to name a few, are sites indicative of the magnificent history and culture of the Middle Kingdom. A walk through Suzhou's Gardens, a hike through the Yellow Mountain, or a boat ride down the Three Gorges will offer the visitor a more leisurely expedition. Traveling through the Middle Kingdom may sometimes be a challenge, but it is always an extremely rewarding one.

This series aims to offer an in-depth look at each of these famous locations, to give the discerning traveler detailed descriptions accompanied by a thorough historical and cultural background. With beautiful illustrations and photographs, you will find our "Travel through the Middle Kingdom" books the most trustworthy companions, and a useful introduction to the wonders of China.

The Tiger Hill

Suzhou Railway Station BeiHuan Rd. (E) BeiHuan Rd. (E)
BeiHuan Rd. (W) CheZhan Rd. PingQi Rd. Outer Moat
Shantang River HuQiu Rd. BeiYuan Rd. DongHuan Rd.
GuangJi Rd. ReMin Rd. QiMen Rd. The Humble Administrator's Garden
XiYuan Rd. GuangJi Rd. The North Temple Pagoda XiBei St. DongBei St. DongBei St.
The West Garden TaoHuaWu St. The Lion Forest Garden
The Lingering Garden BaiTa Rd. (W) The North Semi-Garden The Zoo
Shangtang River LiuYuan Rd. DongZhongShi Rd. BaiTa Rd. (E) The East Garden
FengqQiao Rd. XiZhongShi Rd. WangTianJing Rd. The Temple of Mystery The Couqe's Garden
Shi Rd. The Garden of Cultivation ZhonJie Rd. ReMin Rd. Cang St.
JinMen Rd. Chang Xu Rd. The Mountain Villa with Embracing Beauty GuanQian St. LinDun Rd.
GuangJi Rd. (S) JinMen Rd. JingDe Rd. The Zigzag Garden PingJiang Rd.
YangYu Rd. The Crane Garden The Garden of Arhat
GanJiang Rd. (W) GanJiang Rd. (W) YongJingSt. The Garden of Pleasure GanJiang Rd. (E)
Chang Xu Rd. GanJiang Rd. (E) FengHuang St.
Suzhou Government Suzhou Park MinZhi GongYuan Rd.
SanXiang Rd. SanXiang Rd. DaoQian St. ShiZi St. ShiZi St.
TongJing Rd. (S) LaoShi Rd. SiQian St. ShiZi St. WuSa Rd. WuQuaQiao Rd. ShiQuan Jie
RenMin Rd. ShiQuan Jie DaoQong Rd. ShiQuan Jie The Master of the Nets Garden
LaoDong Rd. XuJiang River PanMen Rd. The Ke Garden ZhuHui Rd.
LaoDong Rd. ZaoShi Rd. XinShi Rd. The Confucius Shrine ZhuHui Rd. ZhuHui Rd. FengMenXi St.
XuJiang Rd. XinShi Rd. The Surging Wave Pavilion NanYuan Rd. The Garden of Sweet-scented Osmanthus
The Panmen Scenic Area RenMin Rd.(S) Outer Moat Outer Moat
PanMen Rd. NanMen Rd. NanMen Rd.
Outer Moat

The Tang Yin's Tomb

The Distribution Plan of Suzhou's Gardens

Guide to Your Itinerary

The Best Seasons for Visiting Suzhou

Located in a north temperate zone, Suzhou features a mild, damp climate with frequent rain. It has four seasons, and is most suitable for a visit from April to October. During this period, the natural scenery is at its best and the markets are full of seasonal produce such as fresh peaches, Biluo Tea and the sweet lotus root.

Tips

1. Avoid weekends and holidays if you can. This popular destination fills up with tourists during the height of the tourist seasons. The beauty of the Suzhou Gardens is best appreciated in solitude, or with few people in the gardens.

2. Most scenic spots in Suzhou are closed after 5:30 pm, even during holidays. Please schedule your itinerary accordingly if you are not traveling with a tour group.

3. An annual azalea fair is held from March to June in the Humble Administrator's Garden. The annual water lily fair is held from July to August in the same garden.

Delicious Foods & Delicacies

Squirrel-shaped Carp Dish

Legend has it that when Qing Emperor Qianlong was touring south of the Yangtze River (Jiangnan), His Majesty happened to come to the Crane Building where he caught sight of a shoal of common carp near the altar. He ordered a chef to make a delicious dish with the carp. Excited by the arrival of the Emperor, the chef immediately went to work concocting something special. Finally, he produced a very unusual dish: carp in the shape of a squirrel, the squirrel holding both its head and tail high. The Emperor was extremely pleased with the dish, and his praise traveled far and wide.

Turtle in White Sauce

Two delicacies of Suzhou are turtle in white sauce and stewed turtle in clear soup. They are eaten in spring and autumn respectively when turtles in spring and in autumn are most nutritious. The turtle is chopped into slices, which is seasoned with Chinese yam, bamboo shoots, fragrant mushrooms and leeks. Ginger salt and wine are added as condiments. After it is cooked, the sauce looks bright and thick and tastes both salty and sweet.

Chicken in Watermelon

This dish has a long history is Suzhou as a seasonal delicacy. A plump and tender hen is put in a hollowed watermelon, then chicken broth, as well as slices of ham, bamboo shoots and mushrooms are added to it. Finally, the watermelon is sealed with its own cover and steamed. A delicious smelling, tasty and tender chicken is the result.

Introduction

"An Urban Forest"

Placed on the UN list of the World Cultural Heritage Sites by UNESCO in 1997, the classic gardens of Suzhou exemplify the best of China's privately owned gardens.

These exquisitely designed gardens can be found throughout the city of Suzhou, a picturesque canal city, offering magnificent places of beauty and reflection in a busy urban landscape. This is the reason that for many hundreds of years, Suzhou has been known as a "paradise on earth" along with Hangzhou, a city in Zhejiang Province that prides itself on the breathtaking beauty of the West Lake.

Since ancient times, numerous literary talents have tried to generalize the features of the Suzhou Gardens, among which the most appropriate might be the term "urban forest". This summarizes the fact that Suzhou's Gardens, while built in an urban area, offer an adventure one could only expect to enjoy in a forest, and offer the ideal combination of two diametrically opposed concepts: city and forest.

What requires close attention, however, is that the symbolic word "forest" refers to more than nature itself, but to China's long held literary tradition of the forest symbolizing a lifestyle removed from worldly temptations, and a mind and spirit freed from social obligations. In ancient China, renowned intellectuals often pursued a secluded life in a forest and thus became known as the "forest residents". These intellectuals' efforts to shun the mundane life, regardless of fame or wealth, and their determination to pursue individual freedom became idealized and emulated by the scholars of later dynasties. As a result, a forest now carries the connotation of a spiritual quest — a defiance of society and an embrace of individuality.

As opposed to the "forest", the "city" is the established symbol of human society. Therefore, the integration of the "city" and the "forest", similar to that of Yin and Yang in the Pattern of Taiji, follows the traditional Chinese view of combining two contradictory forces in a

harmonious complement. Under the influence of this philosophy, China's ancient scholars came up with the innovative idea of building a "forest" in the "city".

The Suzhou Gardens demonstrate the perfect combination of two disparate elements: functionally, residences are living spaces for practical use, whereas gardens are scenic spaces for aesthetical taste. China's ancient residences feature symmetric rectangles or squares, whereas gardens are designed to offer structural variations. The ingenious designs of the Suzhou Gardens successfully integrate these two elements into one remarkable entity. A few examples are studies and serene gazebos for practical use placed inside gardens; constructing courtyards and viewing windows to allow the elements of the garden into residences; tempering the solemn preciseness of a building's symmetry by crafting overhanging eaves and carved columns; or arranging the layout by attaching equal importance to symmetry and variation. The design of "residence" and "garden" demonstrates the creative integration of "city" and "forest".

Therefore, the expression "urban forest" pinpoints the underlying design philosophy for China's classical private gardens.

Planting "Forests" in the City

Reliable historical records reveal that China's classical gardens can be traced back to the Shang Dynasty (11 B.C.), when the royal gardens featured clay hathpace constructions. Originally a site for the royal family to pay homage to their ancestors by offering sacrifices, the hathpace witnessed fundamental change in its function once King Zhou turned it into a recreational place by raising birds and animals. This practice of erecting a hathpace and digging ponds in the center of a garden, followed by expanding the area for raising animals was then copied by emperors in subsequent dynasties.

During Emperor Wu's reign (140-87B.C.) in the Han Dynasty when the nation enjoyed remarkable prosperity and stability, royal gardens reached a new scale and a layout featuring "one pond with three hills" was introduced. The construction of the Shang-lin Yuan on the site of the original Qin Dynasty garden was completed. Spanning hundreds of miles, Shang-lin Yuan

Left: An Imitation Scroll of Dai Jin's "Xie An Touring the East Mountain". Painter: Shen Zhou, Ming Dynasty

had as many as 36 recreational palaces with numerous big ponds, among which was the 10 hectare Taiye Pond. Taiye Pond had three hills to symbolize the legendary mountains on top of a hathpace, and measured more than 45 meters in height. Consequently, the hathpace in gardens was eventually replaced by artificial hills. The digging of ponds and erecting artificial clay hills continued to exert a great influence on the design of China's private gardens in later centuries.

Structurally, private gardens of early times were practically copies of royal gardens. The residence of Xie Lingyun (385-433A.D.), a renowned poet of the Southern Song Dynasty, was surrounded by hills and overlooked the lake. Despite its beautiful location in Shi'ning, Kuaiji County (today's Shangyu in Zhejiang Province), the garden was further enhanced by additional adornment of ponds and artificial hills within the garden. Xie's villa-like garden, along with his landscape poems, served as a model for intellectuals of later generations.

During the heyday of the Tang Dynasty, there emerged countless innovations in garden design as Xie Lingyun's villa-like garden became widely popular. However, court officials, whose duties kept them tethered to the cities, needed a closer location to spend their leisure time. Consequently, the ideal of retreating into the "forest" was eventually replaced by the idea of planting a "forest" in the city.

Bai Juyi (772-846A.D.), a renowned poet of the mid-Tang Dynasty, had his residence built in the City of Luoyang with "one-third as living space" and "isles, ponds, bridges and paths scattered around". He decided to create a forest inside the chaos of a city. Inside this garden, Bai lived a life of a hermit and started composing poems of what he called a "moderate" seclusion. Bai attributed "high seclusion" to those who mentally pursued a life of seclusion while serving as high-ranking officials in the court, "low seclusion" to those who lived a sequestered life in the depths of hills, and "moderate seclusion" to those who, like himself, lived a secluded life in the city while serving as low-ranking officials without serious responsibilities.

During the Tang Dynasty, Prince Qi, Emperor

Portrait of Xie Lingyun

Wang Chuan Scroll (Partial). Painter: Song Xu, Ming Dynasty

Xuanzong's younger brother, built a garden with hills and ponds in his Luoyang residence. Although Bai Juyi failed to build a residential garden that evoked a forest in the city, his work of poetry and his theory of "moderate seclusion" has made an unparalleled contribution to the increasing number of "forests" in the city. Since then, a great many residential gardens featuring mini-forests emerged in major cities of China, all across the southern and northern areas of the Yangtze River, and greatly influenced the gardening design of other East Asian countries like Japan.

A Close Look at the "Urban Forest"

Some of China's quintessential classical gardens have survived hundreds of years of change, and Suzhou is a place where most of these gardens can be found. So far, eight

gardens in Suzhou have been listed as World Heritage Sites, confirming the reputation of a city that has been crowned "heaven" since the Song and Yuan Dynasties.

Suzhou boasts a long history of private garden construction. Gu Pijiang's residential garden was famous in the Jin Dynasty, and during the period of Five Dynasties and Ten Kingdoms, Prince Guangling of Wuyue Kingdom (907-978A.D.) built a picturesque South Garden near Suzhou's educational institutions. Afterwards, many of his subordinates followed suit and soon there was a flurry of garden construction in Suzhou.

In 1117A.D. Emperor Huizong of Song Dynasty began building an artificial hill in Bianjing (today's Kaifeng in He'nan Province) and assigned Zhu Chong, a native inhabitant of Suzhou, and his son to ship Tai Hu (Tai Lake) rocks and a variety of flowers to Bianjing. Both items could only be obtained from regions in the lower Yangtze. Tai Hu rocks, unique to Suzhou and only available from the West Dongting Hill of Tai Lake, are hard and smooth and are full of tiny holes that create interesting, unusual shapes. Bai Juyi once lauded them in his writings as the best kind of rock to admire. Emperor Huizong even went so far as to name and inscribe each of the rocks, one larger than 15 meters was named "Marquis". He had these rocks piled up on a hilltop in his garden with the highest point taking as many as 90 steps to reach. This heralded a new type of garden design: artificial hills piled up with rocks, and the Tai Hu rocks were considered the best rocks for use in the gardens.

From the late Yuan Dynasty until the Ming and Qing Dynasties, Suzhou remained economically prosperous and culturally vital. Abundant resources and beautiful sights attracted a great number of retired officials and intellectuals to gather in the city. The richer ones built their private Xanadus at great expense which helped maintain Suzhou's premier position for residential gardens in all of China. During its heyday, more than 200 residential gardens were recorded across Suzhou.

The gardens of Suzhou, with layouts in service of the secular life as well the life of seclusion, have a complementary contradiction that was regarded as perfect for the literati. Suzhou Gardens are known for being "the winding paths to serenity". Yet, they do not only lead to the serenity of the view, but also to the serenity of the mind. To fully comprehend the subtlety of these gardens, one must experience the "urban forest" of Suzhou in person.

Left:A Scroll on Wang Wei's Poetic Conception. Painter: Chen Guan, Ming Dynasty

The Surging Wave Pavilion
—A Heritage of the Song Dynasty

In Suzhou Gardens, except in the Surging Wave Pavilion, ponds are arranged in the center of the gardens in most cases. Today, many view this as a characteristic feature of Jiangnan water towns, which is inaccurate. In fact, the Surging Wave Pavilion displays the classic design of a Jiangnan water town: a garden surrounded by water.

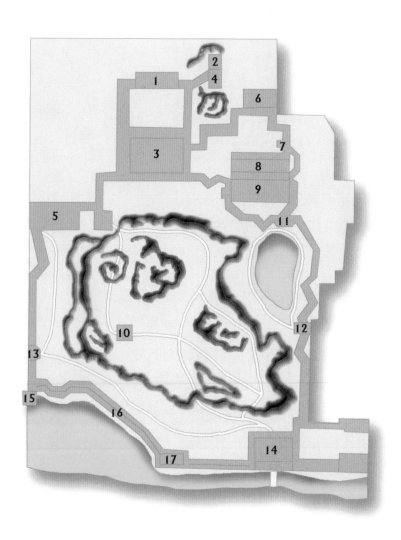

Plan of the Surging Wave Pavilion

1.瑶华境界 Yao Hua Jing Jie (Magnificent Vistas) 2.印心石屋 Yin Xin Shi Wu (The Heart Engraved Stone House) 3.明道堂 Understanding the Way Hall (Ming Dao Tang) 4.看山楼 Kan Shan Lou (The Hill Viewing Building) 5.闻妙香室 Wen Miao Xiang Shi (The Delicate Fragrance Chamber) 6.翠玲珑 Cui Ling Long (The Spot of Emerald Delicateness) 7.仰止亭 Yang Zhi Ting (The Pavilion for Enjoying Beautiful Scenery) 8.五百名贤祠 Wu Bai Ming Xian Ci (The 500 Talented Celebrities Ancestral Hall) 9.清香馆 Qing Xiang Guan (The Delicate Fragrance Hall) 10.沧浪亭 The Surging Wave Pavilion (Cang Lang Ting) 11.步崎亭 Bu Qi Ting (The Strolling Winding Shore Pavilion) 12.御碑亭 Yu Bei Ting (The Royal Inscriptions Pavilion) 13.闲吟亭 (The Leisurely Recital Pavilion) 14.碑记亭 Bei Ji Ting (The Inscriptions Hall) 15.观鱼处 Guan Yu Chu (The Fish Viewing Corner) 16.复廊 Fu Lang (The Double Corridor) 17.面水轩 Mian Shui Xuan (The Facing Water Veranda)

Transport:	Tourists' Coach Line 2, 4 and 5 and Buses No. 1, 14, 28, 30, 51, 101, 102, 103 and 701
Admission:	RMB 10
Business Hours:	8 am-5 pm
Tips:	The Surging Wave Pavilion is the oldest garden in Suzhou. There are 108 types of windows of various patterns and composition in the garden.

The Surging Wave Pavilion surrounded by Water

China's private gardens have always featured ponds as their focal point which explains why garden-building back in the Han Dynasty was called "pond-cultivating" and during the Tang Dynasty, houses with gardens were often called "houses of ponds". This particular feature was maintained through the Ming and Qing dynasties. Thus, most of the Suzhou gardens, with the exception of the Surging Wave Pavilion, feature ponds in the center. Today, many assume that this is the primary feature of Jiangnan water towns, which is inaccurate. In fact, the best example of a classical garden of a water town south of the Yangtze River (Jiangnan)

Ancient Ceremonial Arch outside the Surging Wave Pavilion

滄浪亭

Entrance to The Surging Wave Pavilion

"Forest" made out of Tai Lake rocks.

Zigzag Rockery around the Surging Wave Pavilion

is the Surging Wave Pavilion, a garden surrounded by water on the outside.

The creek in front of the front gate, an urban river during ancient times, once had a span of dozens of square meters at its widest stretch. Today, one end of the creek has formed an inlet encircling the Surging Wave Pavilion on whose shimmering waters the reflections of pavilions and trees are visible. A flat bridge made of granite is suspended over the water leading up to the hallway of the Surging Wave Pavilion.

The east and west walls of the entrance hall are covered with stone carvings narrating the garden's history. The most important figure in the carving is Su Shunqin, a poet of the North Song Dynasty, who is closely linked to the history of the garden. With a history of over 900 years, this garden is one of the oldest gardens in Suzhou.

The garden was at first built during the Wuyue Kingdom, and was later left in ruins. Su Shunqin, a dismissed officer, went to Suzhou and took an instant fancy to the garden. After having the garden remodeled, he built a pavilion beside the water bank and named it the Surging Wave Pavilion, which later became the name of the garden. After Su Shunqin, the Surging Wave

Small Pond under the Rockery of the Surging Wave Pavilion

Pavilion was owned by Han Shizhong, a famous general who won numerous battles against the ethnic Jin army. After that, it was converted into a temple in the Yuan Dynasty and remained a temple until the end of the Ming Dynasty. By the early Qing Dynasty, when the garden was almost in a state of ruin, local officials built a shrine in honor of Su Shunqin. The garden was reconstructed three times by the city government in the years 1695, 1827 and 1873 to what it looks like now.

The sight beyond the hall presents quite a different style, moving from light and shallow water to serene and thick forest. The Surging Wave Pavilion differs from other gardens due to its water feature and its unique location, and some even call it a "real-life forest" so as to distinguish it from those with artificial hills only. The real-looking hills are mostly piled with earth, with stone paths winding upward. The hill lies horizontally from east to west, every peak of which is easily perceived. Topped with lush trees and bushes planted hundred of years ago, the hill offers a spectacular view and the sensation of being in the middle of a forest.

The Renovated Surging Wave Pavilion atop Rockery

The classical gardens of Jiangnan, with Suzhou Gardens as the most quintessential ones, have been named "gardens of freehand landscape", a reference to Chinese artists' freehand brushwork in landscape paintings. This type of painting consists of two parts: paintings characterized by natural brushstrokes, and poems expressing the painter's free will. However, during Su Shunqin's time, painting was seen as mere imitation of nature. Consequently, gardens were seen as a more authentic way to appreciate nature. Many artificial hills were constructed during this time.

The artificial hills, situated in the central part of the garden with its west end adjoining the hallway, make up half of the entire landscape. A hike along the higher level on the west side will reveal a small pond — a heritage of the Song Dynasty — embedded with countless tiny rocks below the steep precipice.

Heading east across the array of old trees, and bamboo in their shade, a square-shaped stone pavilion will emerge on the east side of the hill; this is the very pavilion that gives the garden its name. This Surging Wave Pavilion

was last renovated in the early Qing Dynasty. In the pavilion, a stone table stands in the middle, surrounded by a few circular stone stools for playing chess. All these are artifacts from Emperor Kangxi's era. A few 100-year old trees can be found along the side. The artificial hill is parallel to the Feng Creek outside the garden, and separated by a long walkway. The walkway splits into two parallel smaller ones by a thin wall and is thus called the "double walkway". There are a number of windows on the walls of the walkway to allow a view from both sides. No single pattern is repeated on the windows. There are altogether 108 patterns, and this narrow walkway offers an extraordinary collection of window patterns. This design was so celebrated at the time that it was later imitated in the design of the Lion Forest Garden and the Pleasure Garden.

At the far east end of the double walkway there is a square pavilion surrounded by water on three sides. Its north-eastern location, with the water below at its widest stretch, offers an ideal

Outer Wall of the Double Corridor of The Surging Wave Pavilion

Fish Viewing Corner Viewed from outside the Garden

view of the waters outside the garden, hence the name Fish Viewing Corner. Across from the Fish Viewing Corner, a walkway leads all the way south to the Leisurely Recital Pavilion and the Delicate Fragrance Chamber — along the garden wall.

Veranda Facing Water

The Leisurely Recital Pavilion features stone inscriptions of poems by Emperor Qianlong of the Qing Dynasty. In contrast, the Delicate Fragrance Chamber is a small, exquisite building in the shape of a right angle with its southern part an enclosed courtyard and its northern part at the foot of the hill. Dozens of plum blossoms grow here. The name Delicate Fragrance derives from the pleasant fragrance of the plum blossoms.

Magnificent Vistas

Furnishings inside The Understanding the Way Hall

    Several steps to the west of the Delicate Fragrance Chamber lies the Understanding the Way Hall, the main hall of the Surging Wave Pavilion.

The Understanding the Way Hall's graceful, moderate appearance contrasts with the huge forest-like hills on its north side. To the south of the hall is located a cell named Yao Hua Jing Jie, and several steps to the west brings into sight a small closet above the hilltop. Though its square and straight shape creates an odd appearance, a closer look reveals that it was built of Tai Hu rocks of varying shapes and sizes. Above the square gate hangs a horizontal plaque with four carved characters: Ying Xin Shi Wu. Above the house there stands a small construction named Hill Viewing Building. Traditionally, this location would have been the spot to view the magnificent mountains south of Suzhou, but today, the surrounding high-

The Heart Engraved Stone House

Left: A View of The Hill Viewing Building from The Heart Engraved Stone House

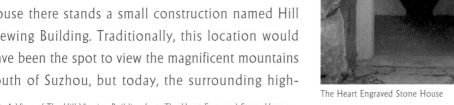

rises make hill viewing just a remote memory. Still, cluster of bamboo in the south of the garden gives some solace. The bamboo is comprised of nearly 20 different varieties.

At the time of the Surging Wave Pavilion's construction, Su Shunqin planted bamboo on the perimeter not just for its a esthetic value, but for its symbol of longevity. Bamboo's straight stems, its ability to endure the roughness of winter, and its knots, all contribute to bamboo's representation of freedom from secular vulgarity. In the Jin Dynasty, there was a group of intellectuals, later known as the "Seven Saints" who gathered amidst bamboo forests. The cultural significance of bamboo became further developed in the Song Dynasty, and bamboo became one of the essential plants in China's classical gardens.

You can only overlook the forest of bamboo from the Hill Viewing Building. To truly appreciate this magnificent bamboo, especially its movement in the wind and its long shadows on the ground, you had better

Spot of Emerald Delicateness

enter the Cui Ling Long, a chamber that consists of three rooms linked diagonally. The rooms zigzag through the bamboo and offer the visitor an exquisite view on both sides, perfectly framed in the diagonal views through the windows. A brief stay in the Cui Ling Long is a refreshing respite, with the emerald bamboo moving to the gentle wind.

Heading north along the winding veranda of the Cui Ling Long, a half-pavilion appears ahead, located at the shrine for 500 respected scholars. A total of 594 stone-carved portraits of well-known intellectuals in Suzhou are to be found on three walls of the shrine. The Delicate Fragrance Hall, comprising five cubicles adjoining one another, is immediately north. This hall is named after the osmanthus blossoms in the front courtyard. North of it sits a tiny stone pond on which Yu Yue, a renowned scholar of the late Qing Dynasty, inscribed the words "Flowing Jade". To the south sits a stone platform half submerged under the water with a half-pavilion. The pond is very small compared to the creek flowing through half of the garden, and the terrace leading to the pavilion was

The 500 Talented Celebrated Ancestral Hall

elevated by the designers to offer a higher level view of the pond. The high perspective creates an illusion of staring down into an abyss.

The central part of the Surging Wave Pavilion is dominated by an earthen hill with a winding terrace. No other artificial constructions can be seen from this vantage point which helped maintain the tranquil and plain appearance of the gardens during the era of the Northern Song Dynasty. The rest of the buildings have been constructed around the hill with the various chambers and halls facing it, a hill-centered layout that follows in the tradition of "lingering for admiration of great hills".

The Master of the Nets Garden
—A Small But Complete Masterpiece

Many of the wooden pillars used in Suzhou Gardens have been damaged by the elements, and it is difficult to find any remaining intact. The residential section of The Master of the Nets Garden, however, still has perfectly preserved wooden pillars, which are a precious rarity.

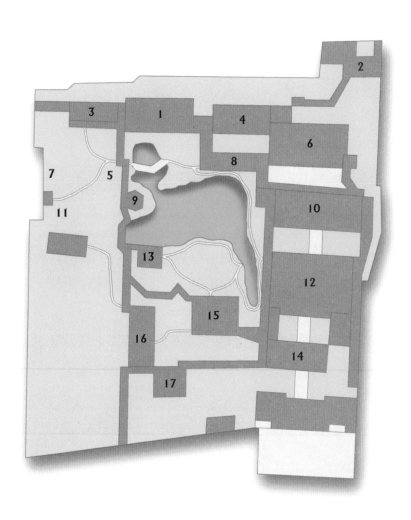

Plan of the Master of the Nets Garden

1.看松读画轩Kan Song Du Hua Xuan (Pine and Painting Viewing Chamber) 2.梯云室Ti Yun Shi (The Hall of Ascending Clouds) 3.殿春簃 Dian Chun Yi (The Spring Worshipping Hall) 4.集虚斋 Ji Xu Zhai (House of Concentrated Abstraction) 5.潭西渔隐 Tan Xi Yu Yin (The Secluded Fisher West Pong) 6.五峰书屋 Wu Feng Shu Wu (The Five Peaks Study) 7.冷泉亭Leng Quan Ting (Cold Spring Pavilion) 8.竹外一枝轩Zhu Wai Yi Zhi Xuan (The Slanting Bamboo Twig Veranda) 9. 月到风来亭 Yue Dao Feng Lai Ting (Moon and Wind Pavilion) 10.撷秀楼（花厅）Xie Xiu Lou (The Hall of Flowers) 11.涵碧泉 Han Bi Quan (Deep Blue Spring) 12.大厅 Da Ting (The Main Hall) 13.濯缨水阁 Zhuo Ying Water Pavilion 14.轿厅Jiao Ting (The Sedan Hall) 15.小小丛桂轩 Xiao Xiao Cong Gui Xuan (Hill and Sweet-scented Osmanthus Trees Chamber) 16.蹈和馆 Dao He Guan (The Peace Observing Hall) 17. 琴室 Qin Shi (The Music Chamber)

Transport:	Tourists' Coach Line 2 and Buses No. 2, 4, 14 and 31
Admission:	RMB 15 (daytime); Night Garden Admission Fare: RMB 60
Business Hours:	8am-5pm; 7:30pm-10pm
Tips:	An Evening Garden Tour is one unusual feature of this garden. Classical entertainment such as Kunju Opera and traditional storytelling are offered. You can view traditional stringed and woodwind Jiangnan instruments such as the Guzheng and bamboo flutes on display in the various halls around the garden.

The Feng Creek in front of the Surging Wave Pavilion runs east past the gate of another well-known garden in Suzhou, the Master of the Nets Garden. Built in 1758, the garden's first owner diverted a stretch of the Feng Creek into the garden, allowing the narrow stream to flow for 700 years, from the Northern Song Dynasty to the Qing Dynasty, between the two gardens.

The Master of the Nets Garden was originally the work of Song Zongyuan of the Qing Dynasty. In Chinese, "Master of the Net" is another name for a fisherman. This name was adopted by Song Zongyuan as a tribute to another garden, Yu Yin, "Fisherman's Garden". During his days as a court officer in Beijing, Song decided to build a residential garden for his mother to spend her dotage, and finally chose the site of a deserted garden once owned by Shi Zhengzhi. After the construction was completed, Song resigned and sequestered himself in the garden until his mother passed away.

Though Song was the original builder of the Master of the Nets Garden, Qu Yuancun, a later owner, was believed to have made the greatest contribution. The Master of the Nets Garden became derelict shortly after Song Zongyuan's death. Qu Yuancun (1741-1808), who passed by it one day, bemoaned its demise and purchased it. He redesigned the layout of the garden, eventually giving it a whole new look. The Master of the Nets Garden today has kept the overall structure laid out by Qu.

Once his construction was finished, Qu pursued the solitary life of a hermit intellectual, in keeping with tradition.

Most of the wood used for the construction of the residential buildings of the Suzhou gardens has suffered deterioration and damage over the years. Very few of the gardens have the residential sections intact. So it is all the more remarkable to visit the Master of the Nets Garden which has a perfectly preserved residential section.

Sedan Hall in the Master of the Nets Garden

The main gate of the garden, like most gates of the literatis' residences, has two huge doors painted black which face each other when opened. There are two small doors to the alleys on the eastern and western sides of the gate. Directly to the north stands a large screen. Four Chinese-Scholar trees were originally placed in front of the gate, but today only two of them survive. The Chinese-Scholar trees planted in front of the main gate is in keeping with Suzhou's long standing garden tradition.

Going straight through the gate hall takes you into the Sedan Hall. The Sedan Hall was a place for sedans, or pedicabs, to be parked and for sedan bearers to rest. The corridor at the farther end of the hall leads to the Main Hall.

A brick-carved gate tower stands between the Sedan Hall and the hallway, both of which were said to be constructions remaining from Song Zongyuan's time with a history of more than 240 years. The tower, known as the "No. 1 Gate Tower of Jiangnan", is famous not only for its long history, but for its exquisite

Ancient Chinese-Scholar Trees Outside the Gate of the Master of the Nets Garden

carvings. Four characters are carved into a stone tablet mounted high on the tower, to assert the owner's "outstanding literary talent and promising future". On each side of the tablet are the historical legends of Jiang Shang of the Zhou Dynasty and Guo Ziyi of the Tang Dynasty. Relief carvings of the lotus root, bats, auspicious clouds and coins are also on the tablet. Jiang Shang and Guo Ziyi are both famous historical figures, while the lotus root

Gate Tower with Brick Inscriptions — often called "The No.1 Gate Tower in Jiangnan"

Inside the Wan Juan Tang (Thousands of Books Hall)

symbolizes fertility and the word "bat" is a homonym for "luck" in Chinese — auspicious symbols used in traditional Chinese folk art.

The small gate behind the Main Hall separates the interior and outer space of the residence. The interior space, just beyond the threshold is named The Flower

Inscribed Stone Plaque on the Back Door of the Thousands of Books Hall

Hall. It features a two-storey building for the exclusive use of the female family members. The Flower Hall, like the Main Hall, has as many as five rooms and a room in the wing. The second floor is where the family members slept and the first floor is where women gathered for parties or banquets.

Behind the Flower Hall, a terrace leads to the backyard, a tiny area walled on three

Inside the Xie Xiu Lou

sides (east, south and west) tucked away among a collection of Tai Hu rocks and pines, bamboo, flowers and trees that artfully expand the space. North of it, a small room named "Cloud Ladder Chamber" faces the backyard. It offers a more extensive view from the narrow courtyard alongside it.

An artificial hill made of odd-shaped Tai Hu rocks stands against the west wall which is three meters high. Shaped to give an impression of being inside a cloudy mist, the hill is hollow in the middle with narrow pathways circling upward to the small gate of the Five Peaks Study, thus giving rise to the name The Hall of Ascending Clouds. An old legend about "picking up the moon on the cloud ladder" originates from this spot. The small climb up the rocks is designed to refresh the hiker as he takes in the sensation of being high up in the clouds.

The Five Peaks Study is one of the five halls in the garden with courtyards both to the south and to the north of it. The bigger southern courtyard in

Above: The Back courtyard as Viewed from the Hall of Ascending Clouds in the South
Below: Tai Hu Rockeries in the Back Courtyard

Backyard of the Master of the Nets Garden

Looking at an Artificial Hill through the Moon Gate

front of the study also features artificial hills made of Tai Hu rocks. Designed as two separate parts, the southern hills present a magnificent spectacle of rolling peaks, while the outer part of the hills, piled high with

Inside the Five-Peak Study

Tai Hu rocks, gives an image of beautiful clouds. The white wall against which the artificial hills stand shines brightly when hit by the sun's rays. A camellia tree stands in the flower terrace at the foot of the hills. Featuring as many as 13 different colored blossoms, it is known as "The Thirteen Guards", and is one of the treasures of the Master of the Nets Garden.

A moon gate behind the study leads to the House of Concentrated Abstractions, a two-storey building used for unmarried girls in ancient times. The house, originally built to refine one's spiritual state, is ascetic and simple, and only two clumps of bamboo serve as ornaments on the terrace. A very special place, this is the spot to forget about worldly troubles.

The residential part that takes up half of the eastern section of the garden ends here. Though a residential construction, Master of the Nets Garden features many courtyards, flower terraces and patios that provide excellent views.

A few paths connect the residential and scenic parts. The first is a gate for the exclusive use of tourists and offers the ideal sightseeing view. The gate is so narrow that, once beyond it, the view expands immediately, giving a feeling of high mountains and expansive waters. Though the Master of the Nets Garden is only one-eighth the size of The Humble Administrator's Garden, its ingenious design

Plaque and Screens inside the Ji Xu Zhai

Cloud Hammock as seen through the North Window of the Hill and Sweet-scented Osmanthus Trees Chamber

and skillful arrangement creates sensations of space. The entrance is also located at the longest diagonal cross-section of the garden; there, a "Cloud Hummock" piled with yellow rocks covers most of an enormous pond that dominates the center of the garden. A small hall is built in front of the hummock to expose only one roof. The repetition of hidden vistas all around the garden creates a sensation of a garden that unwinds forever.

Looking through the window to the Hill and Sweet-scented Osmanthus Trees Chamber

The four long windows on each side offer a splendid panoramic view. To the southwest is a small courtyard, where an artificial hill made of Tai Hu rocks rises horizontally from the east and gently descends to the west. It then continues to stretch to the north. These randomly strewn rocks feature lively shapes of animals in different poses, thus the name, Stones of Twelve Birth Animals. These rocks line a long and narrow flower terrace along the south wall where sweet-scented osmanthus flourish. China's ancient poems used to describe the tranquil elegance of hermits' residences as "teeming with sweet-scented osmanthus", a symbol of seclusion, consistent with the notion of "secluded fisherman" in the Master of the Nets Garden.

The Xiao Shan Cong Gui Xuan faces the small Tai Hu rockery and leans against the big yellow-rock hill. In the center of the north lobby is a square carved window through which one may catch a glimpse of the solemn hummock looming near.

Like the central hill in other gardens, the Cloud Hummock was built around the perimeters of a pond in order to enhance its effect. The view of the hill, as it is reflected in the water, adds to its grandeur. As in other gardens, the shape of the hill imitates a layer of clouds. However, the

Cloud Hummock in the Master of the Nets Garden uses a different material for the hill. Most Jiangnan classical gardens feature smooth white Tai Hu rocks, whereas the Cloud Hummock has sharp yellow rocks. The artisans arranged the rocks to accentuate the severity of the hill, and created uneven contours and a few caves. The beautiful rosy-tinged Cloud Hummock forms a reflection in the water that fluctuates according to the rhythm of the wind and gives a sensation of lively motion, hence the name Colored Cloud Pond.

At the meeting of the Cloud Hummock and the Colored Cloud Pond there is a winding stone path. A stroll on the path enables you to touch the rocks overhead and disturb the tranquil water alongside it.

The stone path connects the Yin Jing Bridge on the east side and the Zhuo Ying Water Pavilion on the west side.

The Yin Jing Bridge spans a tiny brook east of the Cloud Hummock. The brook, only a few inches wide, originates from the eastern end of tiny hills surrounded with sweet-scented osmanthus trees, runs past the Hummock into the south-east corner of the Colored Cloud Pond. Perilous cliffs and steep rocks dominate the banks of the brook, offering an impression of profound depth from a higher level. Yin Jing Bridge, only seven feet long and known as the "three-step bridge", was built in the style of a classical Jiangnan stone arch bridge — with a high arch to facilitate the transportation of vessels beneath it. This highly arched bridge over a tiny brook (so that one stride is enough to reach the opposite bank) is used to set off the contrast between the high hills and the narrow brook.

The Zhuo Ying Water Pavilion stands right beside the Cloud Hummock. It is worth lingering a few moments to admire its reflections in the water.

Beyond the Pavilion there is a terrace along the west wall named Qiao Feng Path. The terrace faces the pond on one side. About half way up the

Right: Moon and Wind Pavilion

terrace, a hexagonal pavilion projects from the pond and hangs high over the water. With its three sides on the water, this is an ideal site to take in the reflection of the moon in the rippling water. The pavilion itself is an important scenic spot; it has an enormous floor mirror set into the back wall of the veranda to reflect the sights of the garden.

A few steps beyond the pavilion to the north, the terrace ends and leads to a winding bridge to the east. The almost square-shaped Colored Cloud Pond has two inlets on its north-west and south-east sides respectively. The south-west inlet cuts through the brook like a tortoise's tail, over which the Yin Jing Bridge is suspended, while the north-west one looks like the head of a tortoise, over which the winding bridge on the far opposite side of the arch bridges hangs. Across the winding bridge there is a protruding rock partly submerged under the water. A small chamber facing Ji Xu Zhai lies further ahead. The small corridor-like chamber links the Duck Hunting Veranda on the east to form a right angle. A moon gate opens in the middle of the west wall that leads to the open well of Ji Xu Zhai. The rectangular open windows that flank both sides of the moon gate show two clumps of emerald bamboo behind, serving as a gateway between the indoor and outdoor scenery.

The small chamber, along with the Duck Hunting Veranda on the east of the pond as well as the half-pavilion on the south, is part of an open complex facing the water. The chambers, veranda and pavilions are in an orderly array. Its location, alongside the wall that separates the residential section from the scenic parts of the

Zhuo Ying Water Pavilion

View of Moon and Wind Pavilion Across the Pond

garden, offers fascinating views of the Moon and Wind Pavilion and the Zhuo Ying Water Pavilion across the pond. It also artfully conceals the dull walls to create a natural transition from the residence to the gardens. Behind the half-pavilion is the giant eastern wall on the side of Xie Xiu Lou. The name Half-Hill Pavilion stems from its southern yellow-stone peak which was too small for a hill and thus called a "half-hill". A rock slope leads down the half-hill to a pond where a large protruding rock offers a spot for tourists to touch the clean water and view the fish.

The half-hill, after extending south beyond the protruding rock, becomes a steep precipice, leading to the brook where Yin Jing Bridge comes right up to Cloud Hummock. In the northern section of the garden there is a guest study for

Building Complex Consisting of the Slanting Bamboo Twig Chamber, the Duck-Shooting Veranda and Half-Hill Pavilion

admiring calligraphy and paintings. Performances of local operas are also performed in this artistic study known as the Pine and Painting Viewing Chamber. Square windows with carvings are found in the center of the chamber, with rocks and flowers artfully arranged in the tiny courtyard outside to present a perfect view through the window. A small courtyard lies in front of the chamber. Flower terraces of yellow rocks serve as the barriers between the Colored Cloud Pond and the courtyard. Neatly arranged flowers and plants decorate the terrace along with erect pine and cypress trees, among which an 800-year old cypress tree was said to have been planted by the original owner in the Southern Song Dynasty.

An independent courtyard, of a simple and delicate arrangement, lies in the west wing of the chamber. (The Metropolitan Museum of Art in New York has reconstructed a "Ming Garden" in the Museum based on the blueprint of this courtyard.) With the exception of the room in the north, the other three sides have artificial hills. Rocks of varying sizes impart a grand impression of endless hills within the limited space. A peak rises on the southern end above all the others and gently descends both to the east and the west sides to form a col in the south-western corner. A deep pond, named Han Bi Spring, can be found inside the col, thus causing the small pavilion on the north to be named Cold

Spring Worshipping Hall

Spring Pavilion. The spring has underlying channels that connect it to the Colored Cloud Pond. Tiny as the pond is, it follows the same principles of the Colored Cloud Pond: it contrasts with the artificial hills. However, the pond here is used to set off the hills, rather than the hills being used to set off the pond. Careful observation shows that variations within a theme are present everywhere in the Garden.

A black Lingbi boulder, which originates from Qing Mountain in Lingbi County, Anhui Province, stands one and a half metres high in the Cold Spring Pavilion. It looks like a giant eagle spreading its wings. This black and white colored boulder gives out a ringing sound when knocked. Since very few rocks stand as high, the one in the pavilion is a rare treasure. Legend says that it originally belonged to the Peach Blossom Residence of Tang Bohu, a renowned painter of the Ming Dynasty. The central part of the yard is covered with cobblestones that make up various patterns in different colors.

Chen Congzhou, a contemporary gardening master, voiced his admiration for the Master of the Nets Garden, calling it "the best of all Suzhou gardens, and one of the best nationwide, and a classic example of a 'large surpassing garden with compressed intricacy'".

The Couple's Garden Retreat

— A Romantic Story of Sequestered Life

Suzhou was a crowded and prosperous city, and therefore space was always at a premium. Hence, there are more smaller gardens in Suzhou than big ones. Among these small-size gardens, the Couple's Garden Retreat is unique in its name, structure and layout. It offers a welcome contrast to the Master of the Nets Garden's classical style.

Plan of The Couple's Garden Retreat

1.织帘老屋 Zhi Lian Lao Wu (The Textured Curtain Old House) 2.藏书楼 Cang Shu Lou (The Library Building) 3.楼大厅 Lou Da Ting (The Building Hall) 4.储香馆 Chu Xiang Guan (The Fragrance Lingering House) 5.黄石假山 Huang Shi Jia Shan (Yellow-Stone Rockery) 6.城曲草堂 Cheng Qu Cao Tang (The Cheng Qu Thatched Cottage) 7.双照楼Shuang Zhao Lou (The Shuang Zhao Tower) 8.望月亭 Wang Yue Ting (Moon-Viewing Pavilion) 9.长方亭 Chang Fang Ting (The Orthogon Pavilion) 10.方亭 Fang Ting (The Square Pavilion) 11.鹤寿亭 He Shou Ting (The Crane Longevity Pavilion) 12.门楼 Men Lou (The Gate Tower) 13.轿厅 Jiao Ting (The Sedan Hall) 14.载酒堂 Zai Jiu Tang (Wine Storage Hall) 15.群贤堂 Qun Xian Tang (Celebrated Talents Assembly Hall) 16.无俗韵轩 Wu Su Yun Xuan (The Refined Rhythm Chamber) 17.藤花舫 Teng Hua Fang (The Wisteria Boat) 18.山水间 Shan Shui Jian (Landscape Pavilion) 19.魁星阁 Kui Xing Ge (The Star Excellence Pavilion) 20.吾爱亭 Wu Ai Ting (My Love Pavilion) 21.听橹楼 Ting Lu Lou (The Sculling-Beholding Pavilion)

Transport:	Bus No. 701(direct route) or take a *sanlunche* (three-wheeled vehicle) from the Humble Administrator's Garden or the Lion Forest Garden to the East Garden. The fare is RMB5.
Admission:	RMB 25
Business Hours:	8am -5pm
Tips:	The East Garden, the Couple's Garden Retreat and the Zoo are offered as a combination tour. When touring the three gardens, decide on your route beforehand. Start at the gate of the gate of the East Garden to avoid getting lost. After finishing your tour there, you may walk 200 meters along the White Pagoda Road to the west and tour "The Semi-Garden" (Admission: RMB 3). While these gardens are not so well-known, they are very quiet and elegant, and worth a visit.

The Couple's Garden Retreat has three sides facing water, with the eastern side facing the river. With the canal running through both front and back, this garden retains the classical characteristics of Suzhou Jiangnan water towns. The exterior of the Couple's Garden Retreat is the best-preserved in Suzhou.

During its heyday, Suzhou was a crowded and prosperous city. Therefore, many of the Suzhou gardens tend to be small in size. Among these small-size gardens, the Couple's Garden Retreat is noted for its simplicity, as demonstrated in its structure and layout.

"Ou", a word literally denoting two persons laboring together in the field, evolved later to imply couples and spouses. The use of word "Ou" is a pun; it's a play on the word "couple" and the original meaning of a couple laboring together in the field; in this instance, the couple is not quite laboring away, but laboring away to lead a secluded life amid the chaotic turbulence of that time.

Shen Bingcheng, the founder of the Couple's Garden Retreat, was a well-known high-ranking official in the late Qing Dynasty in charge of foreign affairs. Bad luck befell him in his middle-age. Shortly after his father's death, his wife and two children who stayed in Beijing died, one after another. Unable to cope with their deaths, Shen fell ill. After several years of poor health, his health gradually improved, and he remarried again.

Yan Yonghua, Shen's second wife, was not only good at poetry and painting, but was also a woman of courage and intelligence. When she was a young teenage girl, a rebellion suddenly broke out in the county her brother governed, resulting in her brother's death. Surrounded by soldiers, Yan took a risk and climbed over the city wall with her mother on her back to escape.

The courtship of Shen and Yan was said to be predestined because Shen had met Yan Yonghua when she was a young girl and, after coming home, he marveled to his wife about the girl's talent for poetry. His wife even kidded: "If you admire her so much, why not take her as a concubine?" This was to

Side Gate Next to the Canal

come true years later. Following their marriage, the couple started composing poems using matching inkstones and compiled a poetry album together. The love story between Shen and Yan became an often-repeated story among intellectuals of the time.

Having experienced the hardships of life, Shen Bingcheng particularly cherished this new-found relationship and decided to retreat from bureaucratic society. He resigned under the pretext of illness and moved to Suzhou with Yan, where he rebuilt the Couple's Garden Retreat on the site of a garden from the early Qing Dynasty which had gone to waste. Because of this romantic history, the Couple's Garden Retreat has always been considered a place of lovers.

This aspect is revealed in the structural layout of the Couple's Garden Retreat. Unlike other residential gardens that separate residential and scenic parts, the residential part of the Couple's Garden Retreat is in the center of the

Inscription Carved in Brick. Couplets Written by Madame Yan Yonghua, the Wife of the Original Owner

Intricately Carved Brick Gate Tower behind the Antechamber of the Couple's Garden Retreat

garden with two separate gardens situated on the east and west sides, to signify husband and wife. The smaller west garden is a study garden featuring a whole complex of libraries set off by lakes and artificial hills; while the bigger one on the east is a forest garden featuring yellow-rock artificial hills and narrow ponds adorned with pavilions. These two gardens have different focuses, yet complement each other like a husband and wife coming together in the two separate wings of a beautiful butterfly.

This equalitarian notion in the design is quite remarkable for a garden built during this era.

Like the Master of the Nets Garden, a hallway, the Sedan Hall, the Central Hall and the Building Hall are found along the north-south axis of the central residence. However, the front gate of the Couple's Garden Retreat is modest and requires some trouble to find. The existing stone mill outside the gate was recently built and is at odds with the original architectural style. The main gate can be found by a tiny alley next to a canal with a small pier next to the front gate for boats to dock, a characteristic typical of Jiangnan water town gardens.

Tai Hu rocks are strewn casually in the courtyard between the hallway and the sedan hall, offering a glimpse of the garden inside.

The main hall ahead is named the Wine Storage Hall. A horizontal plaque with inscriptions written by Li Hong Yi, the original owner of the Master of the Nets Garden, hangs over the gate. A wall separates the main hall and the stairwell at the back. The wall gate tower has exquisite three-tiered brick carvings of poets gathering together while enjoying wine. The figures are in varying poses, with the inscriptions saying: Shi Jiu Lian Huan (Drink Wine Compose Poems). The only flaw is that the heads of the carved figures in the first two sections have been damaged.

The courtyard in front of the Main Building Hall features two wings, a building on the east and a building on the west, creating a concave layout for the bedrooms of the garden's original owner and his family. A moon gate in the corridor of the west building leads to the western part of the garden.

Inside the Sedan Hall

Inside the Wine-Storage Hall — the Main Hall of the Couple's Garden Retreat

Courtyard outside the Library Building

The architecture of the buildings in the Couple's Garden Retreat has outstanding features. The entire northern part features buildings of dissimilar construction facing different directions, with the second floor interconnected by walkways (nicknamed the Zou Ma Building). Though winding walkways are not uncommon, the Couple's Garden Retreat is the only example of a dozen buildings being interconnected by winding walkways. There is even a hanging walkway from east to west, creating many more viewing angles of the garden.

The western part of the Couple's Garden Retreat has quite a few small rooms and features two buildings: the library building on the north side and the study in the middle. The study divides the western garden into two parts: the southern (front) part that features mainly scenic spots, and the northern (back) part where most buildings are clustered. The northern

Textured Curtain Old House

part slightly adorns the southern part which has lakes, hills and plants. The symbolic significance is further enhanced by a well on the south-west side which corresponds with the water pond in the eastern garden, which is why the name "east pond and west well" came into being. The design of the Couple's Garden Retreat strikes a delicate balance between east and west, and unlike the precise symmetry of western-style gardens, uses a symmetry of reflection and contrasts.

The Library Building of the Couple's Garden Retreat used to have three libraries for books. Though one library has been pulled down, the existing two still remain, giving a sense of the owner's comprehensive original collection.

In the Textured Curtain Old House, an elegant but moderate study was built with folding screens and doors to divide the study into two

parts: the south and the north. The two separate rooms are equipped with different furniture and decorations that complement each other. The Couple's Garden Retreat focuses on correspondence in every aspect in order to replicate marital love, again evident in the structure of the study.

South of the library Building is a scenic spot featuring an artificial hill

Rockery in the West Garden

made from Tai Hu rocks rising from the south-west and descending to the north-east with caves spiraling upwards.

Many 100-year old trees remain on and below the hill to block out the sunshine. A white-painted wall winds around the peak of the hill with a moon gate for visitors to pass through. The walls seem like white clouds drifting around a mountain at first glance, hence the name Cloud Wall. The gracefully shaped lake-rock hill presents a gentle beauty against the Cloud Walls. The feminine beauty of the hill forms a direct contrast with the masculine-style grandeur of the yellow-rock hill in the east garden.

A half-pavilion named "Crane Longevity Pavilion" rests against the wall to the east of the lake-rock hill, offering an ideal view while shielding the side wall of the Sedan Hall.

In the east of the study sits a tiny square pavilion that intersects the scenery in the front and back of the courtyard. This is where the stretch of Tai Hu rockery in the west garden comes to an end. Zigzagging east from the pavilion, you will find yourself back in the central residential part.

There is more than one route into the residential part of the east garden,

Left: Looking through the Window of the Textured Curtain Old House

Carved Window on the Crane Longevity Pavilion

but the best route is through the moon gate on the east side of the hallway. A tiny courtyard comes into view once you go beyond the moon gate.

Traditional aesthetics attached great importance to silent profoundness and implicit representation, and we can see examples of

Stone Stool in the Courtyard of the Lake Stone Peak

this in the Couple's Garden Retreat. The garden remains consistent with the "hidden" notion of everything, from its tucked-away location in the depths of an alley, to the plain-looking front gate, to the entrance courtyard that only reveals part of the scenery. Using the art of contrast, the entrance garden has an exquisite array of Three-peak Lake rocks whose delicateness is further accentuated by the ancient pine trees and several sweet-scented osmanthus trees. The spectacular artificial hill is built up with yellow rocks with sharp contours.

The Refined Rhythm Chamber, nestling on one side of the garden, features elegant furniture and decorations. A short break in the chamber before crossing over to

Courtyard in the East Garden

the east garden promises to purge your spirit of earthly desires and permits you to admire the forest in a more tranquil mood.

The view suddenly expands just beyond the courtyard. Not far away stands a huge yellow-rock hill that seems to have countless peaks. Ancient trees are to be found everywhere upon the hill, and turnips and arrowroots hang from the cliffs, a sight only available in the forest. A long stretch of walkway at the foot of the hill zigzags from the Cheng Qu Thatched Cottage at the north to the Sculling-Beholding Pavilion on the south-eastern side. The walkway along the west corridor connects all the buildings together like a strand inside a pearl necklace.

Unlike most gardens that pay more attention to ponds rather than hills, the Couple's Garden Retreat is centered around artificial hills. The notion of a seclusion for couples is highlighted by the design of the hill, which are

Osmanthus Walkway

divided into eastern and western parts. Likewise, the main hill of the east garden also has two parts linked by a valley known as Sui Valley. Though of a moderate length and wide enough for only one person to pass through,

Sui Valley seems to be a deep abyss thanks to its winding paths and perilous cliffs. The hill on the west side descends from Sui Valley to form a flat slope, with the rest of the hill extending to the walkway of the west wall. In comparison, the hill on the east side rises from Sui Valley to the east and plummets down by the pond to form a precarious cliff overlooking the water. Standing straight and steep, the hill

Waterside Pavilion between the Rainbow-Embracing Bridge and the Landscape Pavilion

presents a formidable appearance compared with the hill on the west side.

Separating the east hill from the west one, Sui Valley also functions as a connecting path for visitors. Heading east along the winding path, you will come to a pond below the cliff. Take your time to stroll around the pond. If you climb upwards on the winding hillside path, you will pass the Cloud-Embracing Cave opposite the pond and below the cliff. Further ahead, the peak can be seen.

On the hilltop, there is no pavilion, just a platform. The platform offers a stone table with stools for a rest. A mixture of grandeur and delicate beauty, the hill presents distinct views from different angles, similar in style to Chinese free-hand stroke painting.

A long and narrow pond named the Moon-Reflecting Pond can be found at the Moon-Viewing Pavilion on the north side. To the south of the pond is a water pavilion called the Landscape Pavilion. With a narrow northern

Looking at the Rainbow-Embracing Bridge and the Landscape Pavilion from the top of the Cloud-Embracing Cave

stretch and a wide southern stretch, the pond is in the shape of an antelope's horn with its tip cut off. Next to the middle section of the pond is the Yellow-Stone Rockery. Spanning the pond is a three-zigzag bridge known as the Rainbow-Embracing Bridge.

The granite slate bridge rises high over the water. The bridges in Suzhou gardens tend to hover close to the water, but the three-zigzag bridge in the Couple's Retreat Garden uses high-suspension to create a deeper effect over the pond.

Afterwards, take your time to appreciate the picturesque view at the water pavilion known as the Landscape Pavilion in the southern part of the pond. Facing the Moon-Reflecting Pond in the north, this delicate square pavilion accommodates the full breadth of the pond. There is a winding veranda in the pavilion, and a small room in the center with walls only on the eastern and western sides, and huge gates on the southern and the eastern sides. Lively patterns of pines, bamboo and plum blossoms, known as "three friends of winter", are engraved in the Zi Qi wood cover, demonstrating excellent craftsmanship. This piece is one of the treasures in the Couple's Garden Retreat.

Looking north from the pavilion, you cannot fathom the actual size of the pond due to the walls on both sides, accentuating the seeming infinity of the water. The pond narrows down at the artificial hill, conveying a sense of remoteness just before the spectacle of the magnificent hill.

On top of the pavilion, other buildings in the east garden dot the central landscape. Fewer buildings are found on the west side, where only the Wisteria Boat and the Fragrance Lingering House stand. The Wisteria Boat, constructed on the eastern side of the Refined Rhythm Chamber, is a not a real boat, and has wisteria growing outside the window. The Fragrance Lingering House was the study for the children of the original owner. The name comes from the lingering scent of osmanthus outside the window.

To the north of the Lingering Fragrance House sits a huge two-storey building, the main feature of the east garden: "Cheng Qu Thatched Cottage."

Exterior of the Wisteria Boat

Cheng Qu Thatched Cottage

Another View of the Inkstone Restoration Chamber

Lattice-Work Screen made from Gingko inside the Inkstone Restoration Chamber

Yun Corridor

The name is an accurate description of the garden's location in the north-eastern corner of the city of Suzhou, with "Cheng Qu" literally meaning "city corner". The three rooms on the ground floor are main halls where the family members held banquets. They also served as the main site for hill-viewing. The window facing south has a terrace that hides the view of the yellow-stone rockery. Shaded by a wide canopy of trees dating back hundreds of years, the terrace has a stone table and stools. Here, you take refuge from the summer's heat.

Go up the stairs to visit the original owner's study. The floor is laid with unpainted fir that absorbs moisture in the air and keeps the room dry — crucial to the preservation of paper. The furnishings give the study an antique appearance.

On the eastern side of Cheng Qu Thatched Cottage sits a small two-storey building that, along with the cottage, was constructed in the shape of

The Star Excellence Pavilion and the Sculling-Beholding Building as Viewed from the Osmanthus Walkway

a right angle to complement the turret in the library at the far western end of the garden. The ground floor is named the Inkstone Restoration Chamber and upstairs, the Shuang Zhao Tower.

The Inkstone Restoration Chamber has incredible woodwork, particularly the rows of long windows that separate one hall from another, featuring lattice-work patterns of flowers and leaves around the frame of each window. The partition plates in the middle and the skirting panels display delicate and fascinating carvings, while delicate craftsmanship can be seen in items such as the door screens. The fine workmanship of the Chamber stands in sharp contrast with the plainness of the Cheng Qu Thatched Cottage.

Beyond the Chamber, you will catch the sight of the Yun Corridor winding along the east wall. Literally, "yun" refers to the fresh bamboo of spring, and fresh bamboo lines the walkway to create a corresponding effect.

Two pavilions rest on both sides of the Yun Corridor: the Moon-Viewing Pavilion to the north and the My Love Pavilion to the south. The two pavilions face each other like lovers, and make a perfect pair. Such harmony can be found everywhere in the garden: the northern building is named Shuang Zhao Tower while the southern one is called the Sculling-Beholding Pavilion.

The Sculling-Beholding Pavilion, standing in the south-eastern nook of the garden, faces water on two sides with a small brook running below the eastern window. Here you can get a taste of the real Jiangnan water-town view outside the garden. West of it is a smaller building of similar shape called the Star Excellence Pavilion. The two buildings are linked by a path on the second floor and a veranda on the ground floor, demonstrating intimacy, like a pair of blossoming lotuses on one stem. They are reflected in the water only yards away from each other, evoking a beautiful image of the couple, Shen and Yan, who lived a peaceful and contented life together in this garden.

The Humble Administrator's Garden

— A Classical Example of a Master-Style Garden

While most Suzhou gardens are small and delicate, the Humble Administrator's Garden stands out as a garden on a grand scale. It is often included in the list of the four most famous gardens in China, the other three being the Summer Palace in Beijing, the Chengde Summer Resort north of Beijing, and the Lingering Garden of Suzhou. The four most famous gardens in Suzhou represent the great gardening philosophies of the Song, Yuan, Ming and Qing Dynasties (the Surging Wave Pavilion, the Lion Forest Garden, the Humble Administrator's Garden and the Lingering Garden respectively). Only the Humble Administrator's Garden makes both lists.

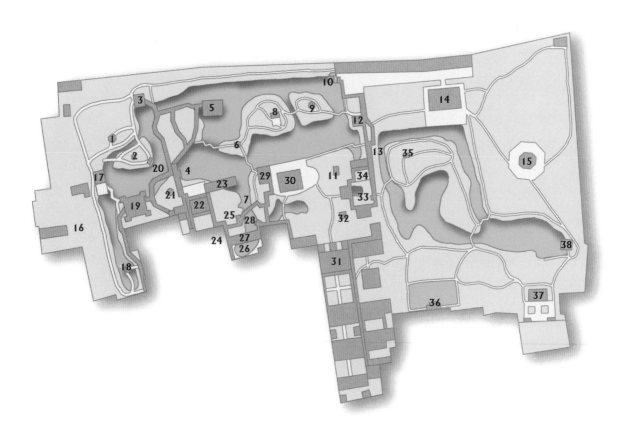

Plan of the Humble Administrator's Garden

1.浮翠阁 Fu Cui Ge (The Floating Green Pavilion) 2.笠亭 Li Ting (The Bamboo Hat Pavilion) 3.倒影楼 Dao Ying Lou (Reflection Building) 4.别有洞天 Bie You Dong Tian (A Different World) 5.见山楼 Jian Shan Lou (Mountain-Viewing Building) 6.荷风四面亭 He Feng Si Mian Ting (The Water Lily Square Pavilion) 7.小飞虹 Xiao Fei Hong (The Little Flying Rainbow) 8.雪香云蔚亭 Xue Xiang Yun Wei Ting (The Snowy Fragrance and Floating Clouds Pavilion) 9.待霜亭 Dai Shuang Ting (The Awaiting Frost Pavilion) 10.绿漪亭 Lu Yi Ting (The Green Ripple Pavilion) 11.绣绮亭 Xiu Qi Ting (Embroidered Silk Pavilion) 12.梧竹幽居 Wu Zhu You Ju (Bamboo Sequestered Residence) 13.倚虹亭 Yi Hong Ting (Rainbow Leaning Pavilion) 14.秫香馆 Shu Xiang Guan (The Drifting Fragrance Hall) 15.天泉亭 Tian Quan Ting (The Heaven Spring Pavilion) 16.盆景园 Pen Jing Yuan (The Landscape Pavilion) 17.留听阁 Liu Ting Ge (The Stay and Listen Pavilion) 18.塔影亭 Ta Ying Ting (The Pagoda Shadow Pavilion) 19.三十六鸳鸯馆 十八曼陀罗花馆 San Shi Liu Yuan Yang Guan Shi Ba Man Tuo Luo Hua Guan (The House of 36 Mandarin Ducks and the House of 18 Stramonium Blossoms) 20.扇亭 Shan Ting (The Fan-Shaped Pavilion) 21.宜两亭 Yi Liang Ting (The Dual Suitability Pavilion) 22.玉兰堂 Yu Lan Tang (The Magnolia Hall) 23.香洲 Xiang Zhou (The Aromatic Oasis) 24.志清意远 Zhi Qing Yi Yuan (The Pure Aim and High-Aiming Room) 25.得真亭 De Zhen Ting (The Truth Pavilion) 26.静深亭 Jing Shen Ting (The Deep Silence Pavilion) 27.小沧浪 Xiao Cang Lang (The Little Surging Wave Pavilion) 28.听松风处 Ting Song Feng Chu (The Wind-in-the-Pines Spot) 29.南轩[倚玉轩] Nan Xuan [Yi Yu Xuan] (The South Pavilion [The Jade-Leaning Pavilion]) 30.远香堂 Yuan Xiang Tang (The Drifting Fragrance Hall) 31.园林博物馆 Yuan Lin Bo Wu Guan (The Garden Museum) 32.枇杷园 嘉实亭 Pi Pa Yuan Jia Shi Ting (The Loquat Garden and The Jia Shi Pavilion) 33.听雨轩 Ting Yu Xuan (Listening to the Rain Chamber) 34.海棠春坞 Hai Tang Chun Wu (The Flowering Crabapple Terrace) 35.放眼亭 Fang Yan Ting (The Looking Afar Pavilion) 36.涵青亭 Han Qing Ting (The Green Vista Pavilion) 37.兰雪堂 Lan Xue Tang (The Blue Snow Hall) 38.芙蓉榭 Fu Rong Xie (The Hibiscus Pavilion)

Transport:	Tourists' Coach Line 1, 2 and 5 and Buses No. 2 and 3. Get off at the stop for the Humble Administrator's Garden and then walk east 100 meters.
Admission:	RMB 45 (slightly more during the Rhododendron Fair or Water Lily Fair seasons), RMB 10 for the Royal Prince House.
Business Hours:	8:15am- 4:15 pm
Tips:	A portable e-guide can be rented at the entrance. After you leave the Humble Administrator's Garden, a 100 meters' walk to the west will take you to the Royal Prince House of the Tai Ping Heavenly Kingdom, the Suzhou Museum, and the Suzhou Gardens Museum. Walk another 100 meters south along the Garden Road to get to the Lion Forest Garden and the Suzhou Folk Culture Museum.

While most Suzhou gardens are small and delicate, the Humble Administrator's Garden stands out as a garden on a grand scale. It is often included in the list of the four most famous gardens in China, the other three being the Summer Palace in Beijing, the Chengde Summer Resort north of Beijing, and the Lingering Garden of Suzhou. The four most famous gardens in Suzhou represent the great gardening philosophies of the Song, Yuan, Ming and Qing Dynasties (the Surging Wave Pavilion, the Lion Forest Garden, the Humble Administrator's Garden and the Lingering Garden respectively). Only the Humble Administrator's Garden makes both lists.

A classic example of a Ming garden in Suzhou, the Humble Administrator's Garden was constructed in the 9th year of Emperor Jiajing's rule in the Ming Dynasty (A.D.1530) and attracted the attention of Wen Zhengming, the leading figure of the Wumen Painting Genre, from the very beginning of its construction.

Wen had, five times in a row, worked on a painting of the garden, and his collection of 31 "Eulogistic Paintings of the Humble Administrator's Garden", completed in 1533 in his third artistic attempt, remains intact today. Wen's eulogy made the garden famous, and it soon became the most famous garden in Suzhou. In 1631, the eastern part of the garden was sold by the owner and later reconstructed as the Field Return Garden. The remaining part of the garden started to deteriorate until another owner took possession of the garden in the early Qing Dynasty, and started to restore its original grandeur. Wu Weiye, the leading poet in the early Qing Dynasty, composed a long poem to eulogize the camellias in the garden.

Although having been left to ruins for years, the garden was not beyond restoration. However, it seemed fated to experience more hardships, as two of its subsequent owners were convicted of serious crimes, leading to its seizure by the government both times. Consequently, the garden suffered much damage. In 1736, the central and western parts of the garden were in the hands of two owners, and the garden was in three separate sections. During the turbulent era of the Tai Ping Heavenly Kingdom, Li Xiucheng combined the central and western parts to build a residence for himself and then started to restore the garden. When the Tai Ping Heavenly Kingdom was toppled, the western part returned to the hands of the original owner, and the garden again separated into three parts, with the central part converted into the official residence of the Jiangsu Governor. When Zhang Zhiwan was appointed to the post of Jiangsu Governor in 1872, he had the central part of the garden reconstructed, and commissioned twelve paintings known as the "Wu Garden Paintings".

Today, the Humble Administrator's garden still has the original layout during the days of the "Wu Garden". The western part was acquired by a wealthy merchant in 1877 and, after reconstruction, was renamed the "Bu Garden". But the eastern part was left

The Graceful and Beautiful Humble Administrator's Garden

derelict for years. It was not until the foundation of the People's Republic of China in 1949 that the central and western parts of the garden finally came together with the eastern part to create one complete garden. It was only then that the Humble Administrator's Garden regained its former glory which had been lost for hundreds of years.

Steep Rockery in the Courtyard

However, after more than 380 years of division, the three sections of the garden were very dissimilar in appearance. Only the central part stayed true to the essence of the Ming Dynasty garden, while the western part reflected the late Qing Dynasty aesthetic. The eastern section was the worst yet, almost in a state of ruin, until it was restored.

There was a main entrance to the central part of the garden, but another gate has been built on the eastern side. The tour starts at the new gate, beginning at the east garden.

The east garden was constructed on a ruined site during the 1950s. To rebuild the garden, the artisans took notes from the Gui Tian Garden of the late Ming Dynasty to arrange the scenic spots and name the features. However, the overall effect does not correspond to the artistic and intellectual idea of a classical landscaped garden.

One of the spots worthy of attention is the Cloud-Adorned Peak. The peak is located above the hill behind the Blue Snow Hall to the east of the gate. Standing more than six meters high, the peak features Tai Hu rocks of various shapes and sizes and rises artfully above the surrounding trees and foliage. Built by Chen Siyun, a prestigious rock-positioning master of the

Left: Long Covered Walkway in the Humble Administrator's Garden

The Magnificent Cloud-Adorned Peak

late Ming Dynasty, who used the great painting of Zhao Mengfu as a blueprint (a renowned painter of the late Yuan Dynasty), the peak nonetheless collapsed unexpectedly in 1943 after 300 years of existence. The rocks were repositioned by modern experts based on its original appearance, and offer the only authentic Ming Dynasty element in the east garden.

A terrace runs north-south along the western part, where a small pavilion sits in the middle. A moon gate leads to the central part of the garden. Once beyond the moon gate, you will get an immediate panoramic view of the central garden which is quite contrary to the traditional garden philosophy of hidden views and subtle unveiling. Thus, the central garden was initially dismissed as a complete failure when the east garden was undergoing construction.

Typically, a visit to a Jiangnan garden is supposed to begin with a stroll through the residential area. Unfortunately, because the original layout of the Humble Administrator's Garden was destroyed by its turbulent history, it is not possible in this garden. Zhang Zhiwan reconstructed the central part with a moon gate as the garden entrance. This gate can still be found today, not too far from the street, with brick carvings bearing three characters (Zhuo Zheng Yuan拙政园) "Humble Administrator's Garden" in ancient Li Shu, Li-style calligraphy. Beyond the gate, you will find on both sides narrow lanes with huge gables that lead to the central part of the garden.

View of the Drifting Fragrance Hall when the Water Lilies are in blossom

A yellow-stone hill of strange appearance is the first sight that catches your attention. With a variety of trees thriving on its hilltop, the hill is an ideal scenic barrier to create the unfolding scene. A creek runs along the northern side of the hill. A stone bridge goes over it. Take a stroll along the winding veranda and the scenery unfolds slowly just like a scroll painting. The view does not expand until you reach the northern platform of the Drifting Fragrance Hall, where the entire central part is dominated by a pond that, together with the exuberance of the rockery, brings out the true grandeur of the garden.

The huge Drifting Fragrance Hall, as the main hall of the central section, has paths winding around each side. The hall has no walls, just pillars and windows, to allow exquisite views of the entire central section.

Snowy Fragrance and Floating Clouds Pavilion

To the north of the hall is a wide porch, and in front of it a large rectangular water lily pond. From the porch, the misty pond seems to expand infinitely, with three islets stretched across the middle.

The Humble Administrator's Garden features water as the central focus in both the central and western section, where rare flowers such as Florists Cineraria (water lily) and White Lotus can be found. In the eulogistic works of the Song Dynasty's moralists, water lily carries the significance of being "free from the stain of mud", a quality that many scholars aspired to.

On the western side of Drifting Fragrance Hall, a small pavilion leads to a five-turn zigzag bridge, which then leads into one of the three islets in the pond. This islet and the one next to it are often mistaken as one because of their close proximity. However, each of the islets has its own pavilion, which symbolize the three legendary fairy islands of the Penglai. The islets offer the perfect site for viewing the water lilies. Two of the bridges lead to other scenic spots, one a five-turn zigzag bridge and the other a three-turn zigzag bridge. They are both very close to the water, offering the heavenly experience of walking along the water while brushing against water lilies on the side.

The central island that links the islets has a rockery with different elevation levels. Perched on top of it, a pavilion on the east side offers yet another superb view of the water lilies. This pavilion was built primarily for the viewing of plum blossoms, hence the name "Floating Clouds", reflecting the fragrance of plum blossoms which were often referred to as "aromatic snow". The central and eastern islands are linked by a tiny stone bridge.

Planted with lush wisteria vines, the eastern island stands at a higher elevation than the others. Yellow stones of varying sizes form a cliff in the lower part, while a mud hill forms the upper part. A pavilion on the hilltop named "Awaiting Frost" has orange trees planted around it. The famed orange trees of Suzhou can be viewed from this pavilion, and give much pleasure in the autumn when the fruit take on a bright hue.

The islands and pavilions are mostly arranged in order of height from east to west, and are known as the perfect sites to enjoy the water lilies, plum blossoms and oranges during summer, spring and autumn respectively. Known for their different implications, plum blossoms are one of the "three friends of winter", whereas water lilies are regarded as "the most dignified flower" by moralists. Oranges are described in verse by Qu Yuan, a great poet of ancient China, as "aesthetically and ideologically valuable." The ability to enjoy this precious sight in the water's reflection adds to the delight.

The pond and three islets create the main sights of the central section, with the architectural elements built around them. Aromatic Oasis and Embroidered Silk Pavilion sit on the southwestern and southeastern side of the pond respectively, with the Drifting Fragrance Hall — the main pavilion — in the middle.

The Aromatic Oasis is shaped like a boat with three sides touching the water. It functions as an open-water pavilion with a terrace at the front. A brief visit inside gives the sensation of being inside a real ship's cabin.

On the south-eastern side there is a pavilion named the Embroidered Silk Pavilion, which is built in symmetry with the Aromatic Oasis. Built above a yellow-stone hill, it is more than a viewing site, as it functions as a scenic barrier to protect the loquat garden to the south.

Three-Turn Zigzag Bridge Leading to the Islet of the Awaiting Frost Pavilion

Aromatic Oasis Imitating a Large Boat

China's ancient artisans were good at creating multi-layered spaces through a layout technique dubbed "garden-of-garden". The Humble Administrator's Garden is particularly demonstrative of this technique, for it not only has a garden-of-garden layout on both the left and right sides, but also references to contrasting themes from rhymed poems to accentuate the distinct characteristics of the two sides.

A residential complex on the east side features a garden that covers most of the area: the Loquat Garden. Standing between the Embroidered Silk Pavilion and the huge Yellow-Stone Rockery in the south, the garden is separated from the main garden by a Cloud Wall. A moon gate, tucked behind the cliff, leads into the residential garden. The Jia Shi Pavilion, nestled inside the Loquat Garden, allows for the ideal viewing of golden ripe fruit.

Bamboo is planted alongside the Dainty Hall (Ling Long Guan) in the north of the garden. Behind the hall, a porch leads to the Flowering Crabapple Terrace on the left and Listening to the Rain Chamber on the right.

The Flowering Crabapple Terrace is an enclosed study shaped like a courtyard that features crabapples, and flagstone patterns of green, red and white cobblestones laid in a crabapple pattern. Since the delicate flowers do not last long, they were planted alongside the perennial bamboo and Nan Tian bamboo to set off their glaring redness — "cherish the spring" — thereby honoring the short blossoming days of the flowers.

The Listening to the Rain Chamber presents a completely different view: a small creek flowing into the courtyard with water lilies, banana trees and bamboo. This scenery enhances your aural pleasure while providing a place of retreat. The sound of wind and rain was regarded by China's scholars as heavenly music that mirrored nature. And the pattering sound of raindrops on water lily leaves has often been eulogized by poets. It can be imagined that on rainy days a natural symphony takes place in this courtyard.

The Dainty Hall, the Flowering Crabapple Terrace and the Listening to the Rain Chamber are positioned geographically to form the Chinese character Pin (品). A winding terrace links them to one another, and their sights are different, yet complementary: the bamboo forest by the Dainty Hall stays green the year round; the Flowering Crabapple Terrace emphasizes the short days of spring; the Listening to the Rain Chamber underlines the loneliness of autumn. This ingenious design makes the trio akin to a three-dimensional painting, or picturesque verse.

Meanwhile, the sceneries in the western nook opposite the courtyard present a different sight altogether. While the cliffs and walls at the entrance of the Loquat Garden create an impression of being in the depths of a forest, the western nook forms a water court with its inlet

Inside the Dainty Hall (Ling Long Guan)

flowing into an enormous pond.

The path that leads to the water pavilion is a stone bridge named Little Flying Rainbow. Across the bridge there are two small pavilions on the inlet. The first one is named "Wind-in-the-Pines Spot". Surrounded by giant pine trees, the pavilion is an ideal place to appreciate the sound of wind rustling through the trees.

Beyond the inlet, a tiny Surging Wave Pavilion sits over the water and faces a small pond from its southern window. From its northern corridor, it looks over deep and surging water. The wooden pillars on the right and

The Only Covered Bridge in Suzhou Gardens–The Little Flying Rainbow

left of the pavilion are both partly immersed in water, a typical feature of a Jiangnan water town.

The small room beside the tiny Surging Wave Pavilion offers a transitional pathway from the water to the land. Not far to the north is an enclosed courtyard. A mammoth building stands in the middle, built in honor of Wen Zhengming who made important contributions at the time of the garden's construction. The name Magnolia Hall was taken from Wen's residence at the time.

Graceful Furnishings of the Pure Aim and High-Aiming Room

North of the Magnolia Hall stands a half-pavilion "A Different World" on the opposite side of the Rainbow Leaning Pavilion. The half-pavilion and Rainbow Leaning Pavilion are located

Wind-in-the Pines Spot

in the western section of the central garden. Follow the existing route and you will find your way into the central part through the Rainbow Leaning Pavilion.

The Rainbow Leaning Pavilion is a small inlet that stretches deep into the Flowering Crabapple Terrace with a tiny stone bridge spanning the entire inlet. As one of the few remaining relics of the Ming Dynasty, the bridge merits close attention to its variegated stone carvings. Looking ahead from the pavilion, you will find the enormous pond extends as far as the half-pavilion. A moon gate leads to the western part. Behind it, you can see the Bei Si Pagoda in the distance. Due to the limited space in China's gardens, great emphasis has always been attached to "borrowing the scenery" from the outside. The view of the old pagoda in the distance is "borrowed" and integrated as part of the garden design. The reflection of the pagoda in the water creates harmony with the rest of the garden — a classical example of "borrowing scenery".

Lotus Root Fragrance Pavilion and the Mountain-Viewing Building

The buildings in the central garden are mostly found along the south of the pond, while just a few buildings lie to the north. Heading north past the Bamboo Sequestered Residence, you can reach the Green Ripple Pavilion in the north-eastern corner.

The Wu Bamboo Sequestered Residence is an exquisite square pavilion. A few moon gates separate the inner and outer parts, presenting an interesting staggered view of moon gates from a distance.

A complete countryside image can be seen outside the Green Ripple Pavilion. Walking along the gravel path beyond the pavilion, you will not see any buildings until a three-turn zigzag bridge comes into sight at the end of the pond. A building emerges, but stairs are absent between the first and the second floors of this hill-viewing building constructed in the late Ming Dynasty. Instead, a slope-like stair using lake rocks can be found along the western

Willow Shade and Zigzag Road Covered Walkway

wall for visitors to climb. The first floor offers great views of the water lotuses, while the second floor overlooks the hill. Meanwhile, this building is the only piece of architecture at the north-western corner of the garden.

Down the stairs and through the covered walkway takes you to a pavilion named A Different World. The name refers to the Buddhist notion of a network of caves where holy images are kept. Featuring a moon gate that leads to the western part, this pavilion was rebuilt as an addition to the original garden by a rich merchant, and is stylistically different from the elegant central part.

The focus of the western section, which is only half the size of the central garden, is around a pond. Several islets lie in the middle of the pond. Though the pond and the islets are smaller than those in the central part, the layout displays more artistry.

An open walkway comes into sight once you go through the moon gate at the western section of A Different World. The winding walkway faces the pond from the north and joins an artificial hill in the south, separated by a Cloud Wall with a tiny pavilion on top. The pavilion offers a great site to overlook both the central and western gardens, hence its name Dual Suitability.

The two-room hall in the western part employs a novel design with square rooms in each corner with huge windows made up of alternating diamond-shaped purple glass, and transparent glass characteristic of late Qing Dynasty. The hall is divided into southern and northern parts by lattice screens made from gingko wood. Facing the water lily pond and the islets, the northern section of the room offers a grand view, and is the most important viewing site. The name of the hall "House of 36 Mandarin Ducks" comes from a literary quotation from Huo Guang, a renowned government official of the Han Dynasty who once raised 33 pairs of mandarin ducks in his pond. The name of the southern section, House of 18

Cloud Wall Separates the Middle Section from the West Section of the Dual Suitability Pavilion

Northern Chamber of "The House of 36 Mandarin Ducks"

Stramonium Blossoms, was also inspired by the historical record that 18 precious camellias were planted in the southern courtyard at the beginning of its construction. The Humble Administrator's Garden was once famous in the early Qing Dynasty for its "pearl camellias" inspiring Wu Meicun, the leading poet of that time, to compose long verses. Although this precious strain has been extinct for years, it generated huge fame for the garden, which explains why the owner spared no cost in obtaining various precious camellias when he rebuilt the garden. Though the blossoms in the garden are not as rare as the blossoms of centuries past, they still offer an effective reminder.

Heading west takes you along a path to the Stay and Listen Pavilion. Facing water on two sides, the Stay and Listen Pavilion is north of the creek and opposite the double-room. A delicately designed water pavilion,

Sitting-with-Whom Pavilion Overlapping with the Bamboo Hat Pavilion

the Stay and Listen Pavilion boasts delicate gingko wood lattice work with carvings of pines, bamboo, plum blossoms and sparrows, as well as twelve carvings of dragons in clouds on cedar wood, all masterpieces from the Qing Dynasty.

To the east of the Stay and Listen Pavilion is a small islet in the pond. Shaped like a triangle, the islet has two bridges spanning the pond in two directions, one leading to the pavilion and the other to the hill in the north. On the islet is a small round pavilion, named the Bamboo Hat Pavilion for its physical likeness to bamboo hats.

Across the water from the Bamboo Hat Pavilion there is a half-open pavilion, with its windows, doors, stone table and stools in the shape of a fan. Its open windows face the Bamboo Hat Pavilion to the north, and face A

The Undulating Wave-Like Corridor "Swimming Like a Dragon"

Different World to the south, protruding into the water.

An artificial hill stands at the southern tip of the islet, facing the Bamboo Hat Pavilion across a creek. A two-storey octagonal pavilion named the "Floating Green Pavilion", a reference to distant mountains, sits on the hilltop, the highest viewing site of the western garden. With windows on each side, the Floating Green Pavilion offers an ideal view of all the western garden scenes.

Climbing down from the pavilion to the foot of the pond, a two-storey building named the Reflection Building joins a long walkway to the east. The walkway is an odd shape, breaking unexpectedly from the wall and turning into a bending bridge across the pond. The walkway, while flat on the ground, moves up and down on the water, undulating like a dragon swimming above the water. The "dragon", with its tail pointing to the Reflection Building, further

The Reflection Building and the Corridor along the Water

Floating Green Pavilion

extends its undulating body to A Different World, where it finally joins the open terrace leading to the double-room hall. The hall, in every sense, looks like the head of the "dragon". What seemed like a dull design at the beginning, is suddenly enlivened.

There are quite a few unconventional features in the western garden, from the overall layout to its architectural style, that display excessively artificial affectation in pursuit of creativity, not dissimilar to the poetic styles of the late Tang Dynasty. The garden also features some superbly innovative designs, such as the walkway in the east.

On the whole, the Humble Administrator's Garden combines creative imagination with the least amount of artificial elements to reflect natural beauty. This garden's design is no exception, and is a consummate example of China's classical aesthetics.

The Lion Forest Garden

— A Labyrinth of Artificial Hills with Buddhist Significance

In close vicinity to the Humble Administrator's Garden lies the Lion Forest Garden, both of which, while enjoying equal fame, differ greatly from each other in style. Some regard the Lion Forest Garden as the best example of a Suzhou garden, whereas others dismiss it completely.

Plan of the Lion Forest Garden

1.暗香疏影楼An Xiang Shu Ying Lou (The Light Lingering Fragrance Building) 2.真趣亭[听瀑] Zhen Qu Ting [Ting Pu] (The Pleasure Pavilion [for Hearing Waterfalls]) 3.石舫 Shi Fang (Stone Boat) 4.飞瀑亭[听涛] Fei Pu Ting [Ting Tao] (The Flying Waterfall Pavilion [for Hearing Waves]) 5.湖心亭[观瀑] Hu Xin Ting [Guan Pu] (The Lake Heart Pavilion [for watching waterfalls]) 6.问梅阁 Wen Mei Ge (The Plum-Seeking Pavilion) 7.西部假山 Xi Bu Jia Shan (The Western Rockeries) 8.双香仙馆 Shuang Xiang Xian Guan (Double-Fragrance Celestial House) 9.修竹阁 Xiu Zhu Ge (The Trimmed Bamboo Pavilion) 10.扇亭 Shan Ting (The Fan-Shaped Pavilion) 11.文天祥碑亭 Wen Tian Xiang Bei Ting (The Wen Tianxiang Poetic Inscription Pavilion) 12.古五松园 Gu Wu Song Yuan (The Ancient Five-Pine Garden) 13.揖峰指柏轩 Yi Feng Zhi Bai Xuan (The Chamber of Cypress) 14.花篮厅 Hua Lan Ting (The Flower Basket Hall) 15.见山楼 Jian Shan Lou (The Mountain-Viewing Building) 16.小方厅 Xiao Fang Ting (The Little Square Hall) 17.大假山 Da Jia Shan (The Big Rockery) 18.卧云室 Wo Yun Shi (The Sleeping Cloud Chamber) 19.燕誉堂 Yan Yu Tang (The Hall of the Swallow's Blessing) 20.立雪堂 Li Xue Tang (The Lingering Snow Hall) 21.御碑亭 Yu Bei Ting (The Royal Inscription Hall)

Transport:	Tourists' Coach Line 1, 2 and 5, and Buses No. 2, 3, 40 and 701
Admission:	RMB 15
Business Hours:	8 am-5 pm
Tips:	The Lion Forest Garden is near the Suzhou Folk Culture Museum and the Museum of Banknotes and Coins. You can tour these two places together with the Garden. A 100 meters' walk to the north will take you to the Humble Administrator's Garden.

Emperor Qianlong's Imperial Inscription Plaque

Not too far from the Humble Administrator's Garden lies the Lion Forest Garden. Although both are equally famous, they are stylistically very different. Unlike the Humble Administrator's Garden which receives unanimous admiration, the Lion Forest Garden is controversial, with some regarding it as the best Suzhou garden and others dismissing it completely.

Wei Ze, a famous Buddhist monk from the southern branch in the late Yuan Dynasty, built the Lion Forest Garden, naming it after the Lion Garden of Tian Mu Mountain, Zhejiang Province, where he studied Buddhism. "Forest" in Chinese is a term that Buddhists use to refer to place where they gather and cultivate themselves in accordance with religious doctrines. Therefore, "forest" in Buddhist terminology has the same meaning as a monastery.

In the early Ming Dynasty, the Lion Forest Garden was converted into the Neng Ren Monastery, and the head monk invited two renowned poets and the painters Ni Zan and Xu Ben to create dedicated works in the garden. In the days following the collapse of the Ming dynasty and the rise of the Qing dynasty, the garden was left in a derelict state, until the garden and the surrounding residences were bought by the Bei family and restored in 1917.

The scenic parts in the east side of the garden have the appearance of a Buddhist garden from the Yuan Dynasty. There have been no great alterations made to this part of the garden, although much of the restored architecture is comparatively new. On the contrary, the western part, including such scenic spots as Lake Heart Pavilion, the Stone Boat and the Water Lily Hall, features changes

Grotesque Tai Hu Rocks

and expanded architecture. Therefore, between the east and the west gardens, old and new elements co-exist, the former bearing the quintessential characteristics of the Yuan Dynasty and the latter the new elements, a rare combination in a Suzhou garden. After hundreds of years, the Tai Hu rockeries for which the garden is famous are not only the best-maintained scenery, but evoke a range of opinions, both positive and negative.

The entrance to the garden was once the front gate of the Bei family shrine. Inside, a hallway leads to the main hall of the secondary shrine and two side moon gates lead to the terrace.

Built as a double-room hall, Yan Yu Tang has a horizontal plaque inscribed with the characters bearing its name. The wooden screen under the plaque bears the record of the garden's reconstruction composed by the owner Bei Renyuan. Behind the hall there is another courtyard, and across it, a half-pavilion. The porch on the western side of the pavilion has a bottle-shaped moon gate that leads to the artificial hills. Once you step through the moon gate, steep cliffs immediately loom large, providing an impression of the spectacular view to come.

Sixteen huge ground windows with a lattice pattern of flowering crabapples constitute the facade of the front hall. The porch in front of the hall features wood balustrades with carvings of the phoenix and peonies. Stone plaques hang on each side of the porch, inscribed with the Chinese characters "Dun Zong" and "Mu Zu" to show the hall as a family shrine.

Behind the front hall there is a secondary hall, a back hall, and the owner's residence, all of which have been turned into the Suzhou Folk Culture Museum.

Furnishings in the Main Hall of the Lion Forest Garden

Heading west out from the front hall, a moon gate leads to an elegant courtyard.

An enclosed square flower courtyard piled with Tai Hu rocks has peonies blossoming on its southern side. Facing the courtyard is the main hall of the Lion Forest Garden, Yan Yu Tang.

A tiny square hall behind the pavilion has huge open rectangular windows on both its left and right side. Out past the eastern window is a tiny square courtyard where calyx canthuses present an elegant view. The western window faces the hills. Though eclipsed by the perilous cliffs beyond the moon gate, this view hints at the scenery to come.

Beyond the square hall, another courtyard comes into view. In the middle of it is an artificial hill called Nine Lions

Courtyard in front of the Hall of the Swallow's Blessing

Peak, with the rocks in the shape of lions dancing to greet visitors. It is quite difficult to make out nine lions; you must exercise your imagination!

Two Buddhist pines and Longevity Bamboo grow on each side of the hill, in front of which there is a rockery terrace with an array of blossoms and plants. The hill is set off by a white wall behind it on which four stone patterned windows of different shapes — a zither, a chessboard, a book and a painting — can be seen. Also on the wall are the "four literary necessities" — brush, ink-stick, paper and inkstone.

Screen Door of the Hall of the Swallow's Blessing

Lattice Window behind the Nine Lions Peak — Qin (the seven-stringed plucked instrument in some ways similar to the zither)

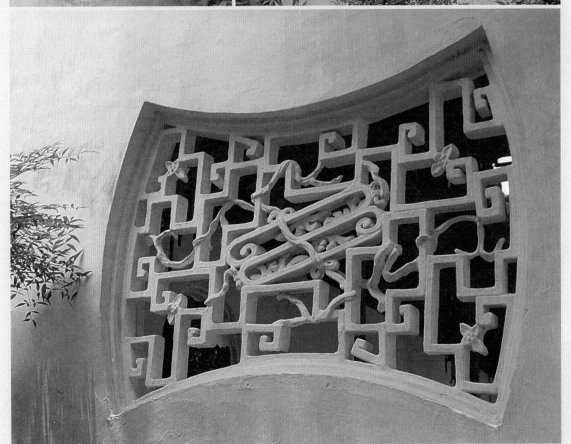

Above Left: Lattice Window behind the Nine Lions Peak — Chinese chess **Above Right:** Lattice Window behind the Nine Lions Peak — Chinese calligraphy **Bottom:** Lattice Window behind the Nine Lions Peak — Chinese painting

Nine Lions Peak

Two half-pavilions built on the eastern and western sides of the courtyard join the winding walkway. The eastern one is small. The one on the west is bigger and enclosed in a pavilion whose flowering crabapple-shaped moon gate on the northern wall makes it difficult to notice. As you enter the half-pavilion on the east, the moon gate, tucked away on the side of the Nine Lions Peak, leads directly into the garden.

Inside View of the Chamber of Cypress

After passing through three courtyards with some minor frustration, we are eventually able to enter the Flowering Crabapple Garden.

The view immediately widens beyond the moon gate. Across the courtyard, a zigzagging walkway by the side wall of the Water Lily Hall leads to yet another moon gate. On the right side of it there is a magnificent two-storey building: the first floor is called the Chamber of the Cypress and the second floor is known as the Rain-Hearing Building. A huge artificial hill, created from rocks of odd shapes and sizes, stand on the left.

The Chamber of the Cypress offers an ideal view of the hill across the terrace. A small rectangular pond sits between the courtyard and the huge hill. A tiny arch bridge in the middle offers a path to the hill. The pond and the bridge, both quite small, contrast sharply with the gargantuan hill behind.

This mammoth hill is the biggest of China's artificial hills. It has nine paths winding upward along with 11 caves tucked away between the numerous odd-shaped rocks. The nine paths, winding through the hill, feature many complicated routes that are difficult to retrace going downhill. A Qing Dynasty traveler reported that he "lost sight of his hiking companion at one time, and found him just beside him the next minute". Climbing this legendary hill is akin to going inside a labyrinth. The hill dates back to the late Yuan Dynasty and is the source of much controversy.

Among the famous figures who voiced their support, Emperor Qianlong of the Qing Dynasty was the most ardent. During his six tours of southern China, he toured the Lion Forest Garden five times. Furthermore, his obsession with the garden led to the construction of two similar gardens in the two royal gardens — Evergreen Garden and Chengde Summer Resort. Yet, disparaging comments were often made by others, as reported in "A Floating Life", a great literary work of the Qing Dynasty: "The Lion Forest Garden, while crowning all the others in Suzhou City, seems to be a messy pile of coal in overall style and totally deficient in its attempt to recreate the magnificence of a forest." Cao Juren, a celebrated modern intellectual, delivered his brief dismissal of the Lion Forest Garden: "It gives me the impression that there are too many artificial rocks piled together, which can only be summed up by the word 'suffocating'."

Contrary to what was standard for other gardens, the Lion Forest Garden never copied scenery from landscape paintings, nor did it use the natural forest as its model. Many of the harshest critics followed these prevailing standards as the sole criterion of an excellent garden. I believe that one can draw a different conclusion and claim that the garden functions as a religious symbol.

According to Buddhism, stubborn obsession is the origin of worldly suffering, and the Nine Consciousnesses governed by one's heart are the contributing factors to the obsession. The hill in the garden happens to have nine paths that wind upward to join at a heart-shaped area on the hilltop, where the Sleeping Cloud Chamber is located. The design is by no means an accident. Wei Ze was most likely trying to express that people have to experience

Poolside Corner of the Big Rockery and The Flower Basket Hall and the Mountain-Viewing Building behind the Pool

countless hardships before breaking the barriers of Nine Consciousnesses to attain a purified spiritual state and be free from earthly temptations. Gao Qi, a poet of the early Ming Dynasty was one of the few who grasped this revelation,

as he eulogized the Sleeping Cloud Chamber in his poems: "Though the clouds are invisible at night and only appear in the morning, my heart shall not change with it."

Poolside Corner of the Big Rockery and the Stone Arch Bridge

Additionally, the artificial hill makes a direct reference to the place where Wei Ze trained to become a monk: the Lion Garden of West Tian Mu Mountain. Wei Ze had a hill erected to symbolize the

The Sleeping-Cloud Chamber Building Deeply Hidden in the Big Rockery

Tian Mu Mountain with a peak shaped to look like a lion. The flat area in the middle symbolizes the plain of a high mountain, hence the name, Sleeping Cloud. The difficult climb up gives the hiker a sense of accomplishment upon reaching this chamber. The design of the building and its name could only have come from a cultivated monk like Wei Ze. Unparalleled in its unique three-tiered and three-dimensional structure, this artificial hill successfully expands the upward space through its twists and turns, an innovation in garden construction during that era. It is also more than 660 years old.

The Sleeping Cloud Chamber is in fact a two-storey building. It stands in a heart-shaped area with the heart tip pointing at a cave. Across the back terrace stands the Yan Yu Tang. This terrace is the sole shortcut in and out of the chamber. On the west side of the hill, a narrow valley goes south towards a water pavilion named the Trimmed Bamboo Pavilion. Straddling a tiny pond, this pavilion has both its southern and northern walls open. Look south to catch a view of the creek dropping down a precipice. Look north to see a tiny rock pond.

The Trimmed Bamboo Pavilion has two gates, with the western gate leading to a lake islet and the eastern one leading to a set of courtyards.

The eastern part of the terrace faces an independent courtyard that has a small hall on its east side named Lingering Snow after an old family hall for worshipping Buddha in the garden.

The Lingering Snow Hall has its western part protruding into the courtyard and features a huge square window on the eastern wall with lattice work on the frames. The window faces the courtyard in front of Yan Yu Tang, and is made more picturesque by the rockery and stalagmites in the courtyard.

The courtyard, as the biggest of the independent yards in the garden, is accessible by a Tai Hu rock staircase under Lacebark Pine on its north. The

Left: Stone Lion with Raised Tail in the Courtyard of the Lingering Snow Hall **Right:** "A Buffalo Eating a Crab" Rock in the Courtyard of the Lingering Snow Hall

ground is paved with cobblestones in the pattern of coins, and a 100-year old Lacebark Pine stands near the western wall with lake rocks of various sizes strewn below it. The taller rock looks like a lion raising its tail, while the shorter one resembles a cow. The cow points its head at another rock resembling a crab with both pincers outstretched, thus forming the scene of a "lion watching a cow attacking a crab". Another rock laying flat on the ground looks like a three-legged toad.

Left: The Elevated Long Corridor of the South Wall **Right:** Fan-Shaped Pavilion at the Wall Corner

Similar to the Lingering Snow Hall to the east, the Trimmed Bamboo Pavilion has a stream on the western side that originates from a big pond.

A path from the east connects the islet and the hill together. There are two other paths, one of which is a trail through a hill of yellow rocks below the cliff, and a stone arched bridge over the pond on the west side.

The rolling hillside along the southern wall takes you to three tiny interconnected pavilions, namely, the Qianlong Imperial Inscription Pavilion, the Wen Tianxiang Poetic Inscription Pavilion and the Fan-Shaped Pavilion, from east to west respectively. The Fan-Shaped Pavilion serves as a viewing site to the north-east garden and is a very pretty spot.

Beyond the pavilion, a long walkway zigzags northward up the hill to an open pavilion named the Double-Fragrance Celestial House. Take your time to enjoy the walk — the northern wall's open paned windows give a good view of the beautiful green bamboo. The artificial hill below leads into the bonsai garden. Plum and sweet-scented osmanthus trees can be found on the northern hilltop, both of which carry a fame of pleasantly sweet fragrance that inspires the name.

Heading north from the Celestial House, a half-terrace stands on the western hill made from Tai Hu rocks and earth collected from dredging the ponds during the reconstruction of the garden. Similar in height to

The Hall of Flowers of the Ancient Five-Pine Garden and the Courtyard outside the Hall

the eastern part, the earthen hill also features three levels. A pavilion with double eaves rests near the western wall of the hill: the Plum-Seeking Pavilion, reconstructed on an old Yuan Dynasty site. During the Yuan Dynasty, there used to be an old plum tree shaped like a resting dragon at this site (planted during the Song Dynasty). Now the new pavilion features patterns of plum blossoms on the ground, as well as a table and stools that are shaped like plum blossoms. A few delicate plum trees can also be found near the hilltop.

The pavilion faces east with a flower hall in the north. In the early Qing Dynasty, five ancient pine trees towered over the hill, thus the name "Five Pine Garden". When Bei started to rebuild the Lion Forest Garden, he had

500-year old pine trees from Hunan Province planted to restore its former appearance, four planted on this hill and the others planted in the courtyard of the Lingering Snow Hall. A plaque with the inscription "Ancient Five Pine Garden" hangs in the Lingering Snow Hall.

Heading north from the pavilion, you will find the Flying Waterfall Pavilion, with a small cascading waterfall behind it. Farther north, the walkway swerves east into a hilltop pavilion. Stairs lead to the terrace below, with the alternative path taking you through the caves. Below, at the south-west corner of the pond, a stone ship comes into view. A complete miniature copy of a Yuan

Stone Boat

The Nine-Turn Zigzag Bridge and the Lake Heart Pavilion

Pleasure Pavilion

Dynasty ship, it is an intimidating sight on the small pond. Looking out from the top deck, you can see a nine-turn zigzag bridge.

To the east of the ship there is the Pleasure Pavilion whose name was inspired by a plaque inscribed with the same words by Emperor Qianlong during his tour of the Lion Forest Garden.

This once magnificent Flower Basket Hall was accidentally burned down and was rebuilt. The terrace that protrudes into the pond from the south hall is situated at the center of the garden, where you can take in the beauty of the water and marvel at the majesty of the distant mountains.

Before saying farewell to the Lion Forest Garden, reflect on the garden's fascinating Buddhist references, and ignore the comments about the "messy" layout of the artificial hill. The nine paths reflect truths hidden in the labyrinth of life, and may take you to higher peaks than the ones presented by the artificial hills.

The Mountain Villa with Embracing Beauty

— A Small Garden of Tall Mountains and Deep Valleys

As equally famous for rockeries as the Lion Forest Garden, the Mountain Villa with Embracing Beauty is located on the west side of Suzhou.

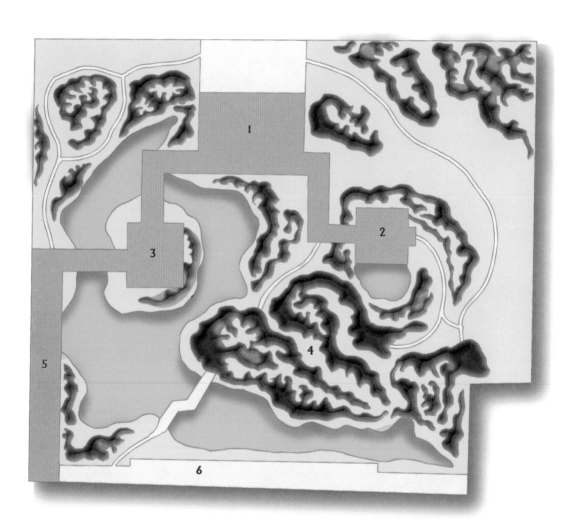

Plan of the Mountain Villa with Embracing Beauty

1. 补秋舫 Bu Qiu Fang (The Making-up-for Autumn Boat) **2.** 半潭秋水一房山 Ban Tan Qiu Shui Yi Fang Shan (The Half Pool's Autumn Water [The Villa Hill]) **3.** 问泉亭 Wen Quan Ting (The Spring-Seeking Pavilion) **4.** 假山 Jia Shan (The Rockery) **5.** 长廊 Chang Lang (The Long Corridor) **6.** 有谷堂 You Gu Tang (The Grain Hall)

Transport:	Tourists' Coach Line 1, and Buses No. 3, 46 and 701
Admission:	RMB 1
Business Hours:	8 am-5 pm
Tips:	A unique scene in the garden is the rockery set by the well-known stone setter Ge Yuliang. Within the space of a foot, you can see an intricate view of thousands of rocks and valleys. Move slowly, and the scenery will change with every movement. Linger here to appreciate the marvelous artistry of Mr. Ge.

The two famous gardens of Suzhou for their artificial mountains are the Mountain Villa with Embracing Beauty and the Lion Forest Garden. The two gardens are complete opposites, yet complement each other. A visit to one garden is incomplete without seeing the other.

The Mountain Villa with Embracing Beauty is located on the western side of Suzhou and was constructed during the Qing Dynasty. Its complement, the Lion Forest Garden, is located on the eastern side of Suzhou and can be traced back to the Yuan Dynasty, and is one of the oldest gardens in Suzhou.

A 500-year gap in history exists between these two gardens. The two gardens also vary greatly in size. The artificial hills of the Lion Forest Garden constitute the biggest existing rockery in China, with the eastern part alone covering more than 1,330 square meters, whereas the Mountain Villa with Embracing Beauty only has a total coverage of 330 square meters. Stylistically, the two gardens cannot be more dissimilar: the Lion Forest Garden features strange labyrinths that symbolize the bewilderment of life, whereas the Mountain Villa garden is a classical example of a traditional Jiangnan style garden.

The rockeries of the Lion Forest Garden are quite unusual, highlighting the grotesque and the magnificent, while those of the Mountain Villa are extraordinary copies of the most famous mountains and valleys of China.

The Mountain Villa with Embracing Beauty is located on the old site of Jin Gu Garden, the residence of Prince Guangling of the Five Dynasties. During Emperor Qianlong's reign (Qing Dynasty), Jiang Ji, the Deputy Minister of the Ministry of Justice, took the villa as his residence, building a study and a rockery beside it. A spring named Flying Snow was discovered in the ground and was later converted into a pond. By the reign of Emperor Jiaqing, Ge Yuliang, a gardening expert, was consulted to create another artificial hill in front of the study building.

Mountain Villa with Embracing Beauty

Spectacular Rockery inside the Mountain Villa.

The garden was then acquired by a man with the surname of Wang during the 21st year of Emperor Daoguang's rule (1841). It was renamed Yi Garden. A hall called You Gu Tang was constructed in the far south with courtyards embellishing the rockeries both in the front and back.

Wang also built a main hall bearing the same name of the garden behind the You Gu Tang. Once, the north side of the main hall faced a stunning rockery in the center of the garden. A beautiful stream, called the Flying Snow Spring, flowed through the middle of the garden.

However, the garden then suffered damage from military raids, typhoons, and various haphazard reconstructions. By the late 20th century, the only remaining scenery in the garden was the Bu Qiu Hillside House. But beginning in 1982, the garden underwent careful restoration to what it looks like today, and is now the exact replica of the original "Yi Garden" constructed during the early years of Emperor Daoguang's rule. Fortunately, the artificial hills created by Ge Yuliang survived the many years of damage and stand largely intact today.

Today, the Mountain Villa has a very simple layout: Mountain Villa Hall to the south and the boat-shaped Bu Qiu Hillside House to the north. An artificial hill lies in the north-eastern section, and the main pond is positioned at the south-western corner. A large rockery in the south protrudes into the pond. Two tiny pavilions with winding paths lead to the Bu Qiu Hillside House. The Spring-Seeking Pavilion on the pond also has a westward terrace that leads to the Bu Qiu Hillside House. A group of uneven buildings overlooking the entire garden can be found along the western wall.

The architecture of the buildings is simple; however, the pond and the rockeries have a more complicated layout. The north-east is dominated by the rockeries while the south-west has a complex of water features, with the rockery of the central garden jutting out into the water. A small island was built on the northern end of the pond with the Seeking Springs Pavilion on

Left: Looking at the Garden through an Opening in the Rockery

Moon-Gate Leading to the Garden

top of the hill. A rockery erected on the old site of the Flying Snow Spring lies to the north-west.

The hill winding along the north-west wall corner serves as a complement to the main rockery with the two hills facing each other across the pond. The cliff on the side that faces the pond has two characters for Flying Snow inscribed on it, an inscription made after the discovery of the spring during Emperor Qianlong's rule in the Qing Dynasty. A secondary path zigzags along the steep rocks and leads through the back hill to the Bu Qiu Hillside House. The main rockery is divided up in the front and back by a creek flowing from the north-west. At the north-eastern corner of the villa, a hill of rocks rises up against the wall, with a hillside pavilion in the middle of it. Physically, the hill has precariously steep cliffs both at the front and back and resembles a pair of wings spread out. This rockery is a magnificent display of rolling peaks, and features countless hidden caves using fewer rocks than expected.

The front and back artificial hills both change their elevation to come to a steep cliff bordering the pond. Rocks were strewn in the creek for the visitors to step on when crossing the water. Covered walkways that connect the peaks of the hills and stone paths both climb uphill and fall downhill to form intersecting paths. Looking down from the peak, the valley seems to be unfathomably deep; looking up, the precarious cliffs seem to stretch straight into the sky.

From time to time, you may pass caves, some of which even offer a stone table and stools. Natural sunlight and wind seeps through, providing a silent moment of pleasure inside the rockery. The rockeries of the Mountain Villa offer the least amount of man-made modification and are the closest to natural scenery.

The tour around the villa usually begins with the entry through the moon gate on the western walkway. Head south along the walkway to reach a three-turn zigzag bridge in the south-west corner. This leads to the front part of the main rockery. Walk along the winding path into the valley to arrive at the front. To cross the deep creek in the valley, use the stepping rocks, but only after passing countless caves along the path. Once beyond the creek, notice the bridge hanging overhead that looks

Looking at the Making-up-for Autumn Boat through the Lattice Window

The Spring-Seeking Pavilion by the Pond

Three-Turn Zigzag Bridge over the Pond

Streams and Valleys Separating the Main Rockery into Two Halves

like it is ready to fly in the air. In the distance is the rock cliff of the Flying Snow Spring. Winding through the caves, the peaks, and then across a bridge, you will then come to the back rockery where a delicate pavilion stands. Take a short break in the pavilion and continue to head down along the pathway until you reach the east gate of the Bu Qiu Hillside House. Go through to the west gate to see the winding path that leads to the Seeking Springs Pavilion in the pond just steps away. The name "Seeking Springs" means visiting an old friend — a visit to the spring is a metaphor for visiting an old friend for a casual chat.

Go west of the Spring-Seeking Pavilion to return to the moon gate at the entrance.

The delicately designed main rockery of the Mountain Villa presents varying picturesque views from different angles. Creating an immense space out of a tiny area, the designer Ge Yuliang truly deserves his reputation as one of the top rockery designers. In addition, the caves in the Mountain Villa do not use stone slabs to support the ceiling, instead using Tai Hu rocks to both fortify the caves and accentuate the realistic effect. Chen Congzhou, a famous garden expert, expressed his admiration for Ge's unique rockery skills, complimenting his skill as "technically advanced and structurally reasonable; capable of creating huge hills with the least amount of rock." Chen delivers a true compliment to the magnificent Mountain Villa, which can only be appreciated after a slow, leisurely visit.

Natural-Looking Cave

The Lingering Garden
— A Surviving Miracle of Superb Rockeries

Of all the gardens in Suzhou, the Lingering Garden, located outside the Chang Gate, is the only one in Suzhou that is a testament to China's tradition of rock collections.

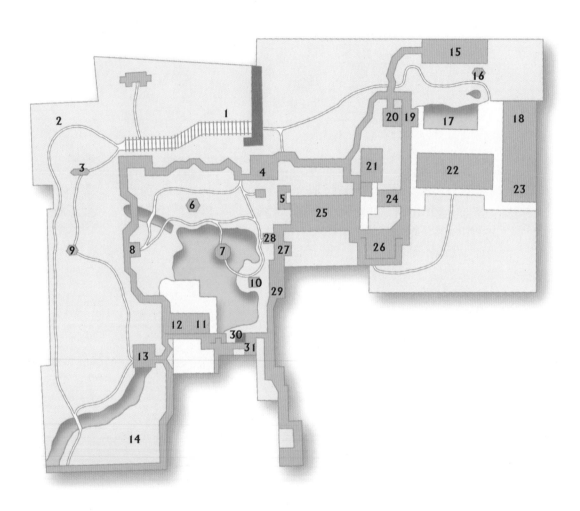

Plan of the Lingering Garden

1. 又一村 You Yi Cun (Another Village) 2. 小桃坞 Xiao Tao Wu (The Small Peach Castle) 3. 至乐亭 Zhi Le Ting (The Bliss Pavilion) 4. 远翠阁 Yuan Cui Ge (The Distant Green Pavilion) 5. 汲古得修绠处 Ji Gu De Xiu Geng Chu (The Learning-from-Ancients Spot) 6. 可亭 Ke Ting (The Ke Pavilion) 7. 小蓬莱 Xiao Peng Lai (The Small Fairy Islet) 8. 闻木樨香轩 Wen Mu Xi Xiang Xuan (Osmanthus Fragrance Pavilion) 9. 舒啸亭 Shu Xiao Ting (The Shu Xiao Pavilion) 10. 濠濮亭 Hao Pu Ting (The Hao Pu Pavilion) 11. 明瑟楼 Ming Se Lou (Ming Se Building) 12. 涵碧山房 Han Bi Shan Fang (The Han Bi Villa) 13. 活泼泼地 Huo Po Po Di (The Lively Water Pavilion) 14. 射圃 She Pu (The Shooting Garden) 15. 冠云楼 Guan Yun Lou (The Cloud-Crowned Building) 16. 冠云亭 Guan Yun Ting (The Cloud-Crowned Pavilion) 17. 浣云沼 Huan Yun Zhao (The Cloud-Washing Swamp) 18. 伫云庵 Zhu Yun An (The Cloud-Storing Nunnery) 19. 冠云台 Guan Yun Tai (The Cloud-Crowned Platform) 20. 佳晴喜雨快雪之亭 Jia Qing Xi Yu Kuai Xue Zhi Ting (Fine-Rainy-Snowy Pavilion) 21. 鹤所 He Suo (The Crane Home) 22. 林泉耆硕之馆 Lin Quan Qi Shuo Zhi Guan (The Forest and Spring Hall) 23. 亦不二亭 Yi Bu Er Ting (The Oncer Pavilion) 24. 还我读书斋 Huan Wo Du Shu Zhai (The Return-Me Study) 25. 五峰仙馆 Wu Feng Xian Guan (The Five-Peak Celestial House) 26. 揖峰轩 Yi Feng Xuan (The Bowing Peak Pavilion) 27. 西楼 Xi Lou (The West Building) 28. 清风池馆 Qing Feng Chi Guan (The Cool Breeze Pond House) 29. 曲谿楼 Qu Xi Lou (The Qu Xi Building) 30. 绿荫轩 Lu Yin Xuan (The Green Shade Chamber) 31. 古木交柯 Gu Mu Jiao Ke (The Ancient Trees Section)

Transport:	**Tourists' Coach Line 1 and 2 and Bus No.11**
Admission:	**RMB 20**
Business Hours:	**7:30 am-5 pm**
Tips:	**The Lingering Garden is divided into four scenic areas: the Middle Area, the East Area, the West Area and the North Area, interconnected by a 700-meter long zigzag corridor. Both sides of the long corridor are adorned with over 300 square meters of stone carvings featuring calligraphy from many dynasties, and are known as the Orthodox Calligraphy Models of the Lingering Garden.**

Of all the gardens in Suzhou, the Lingering Garden, located outside the Chang Gate, is the only one in Suzhou that is a testament to China's tradition of rock collections.

"The Dream of the Red Mansion", one of China's greatest classical novels, is also entitled "The Story of the Stone". Its protagonist Jia Baoyu is also known as a "hard rock".

For more than a thousand years, China's scholars paid special attention to rocks and kept them as objects of admiration and enjoyment. As early as the 6th century, Dao Gai, who served as the Minister of Personnel Affairs at Emperor Wu's court during the Liang Dynasty, placed a Qi Jiang Rock that measured more than five meters in length in front of his residence. During a chess bet on the rock with Emperor Wu, Dao lost the game and the rock was taken by the Emperor to be placed in front of the banquet palace of his royal Hua Lin Garden. The obsession with rocks became even more widespread during the Tang Dynasty. Niu Sengru and Li Deyu, both prime ministers of the middle Tang Dynasty, shared the same fascination with rocks despite their differing political views.

Li Deyu, after placing various rocks around his residence, warned his children not to give away a single one. In the meanwhile, Niu Sengru began classifying the Tai Hu rocks into 12 different classes, even inscribing the details on the back of the rocks. Mi Fu, a renowned painter and calligrapher of the Northern Song Dynasty, searched for "rocks of unique quality". When he found them, he would bow down to the rock. Right through to the Qing Dynasty, the passion for rocks continued. Liu Shu, the founder of the Lingering Garden, was a rock fanatic and the first to create a garden solely dedicated to his obsession.

The Lingering Garden was located at Xu Tai's east garden during Emperor Wanli's reign in the Ming Dynasty. Having been left to ruin, the garden was finally acquired by Liu Shu during the later years of Emperor Qianlong's rule.

Steles of Calligraphy by Famous Poets Displayed in the Lingering Garden

Spectacular Rockeries of the Lingering Garden

Liu rebuilt and expanded the garden and renamed it Cold Green Villa. Liu spread out in the garden 12 famous rocks which he collected throughout China. Later he obtained another five stones and two stalagmites with tiger-hide lines on the columns, and duly placed them in the garden. After a few additional flourishes, the garden was completed.

After his death, the Cold Green Villa became known as Liu Garden, after the owner's name. In the twelfth year of Emperor Tongzhi's rule of the Qing Dynasty (1873), Sheng Kang, the father of Sheng Xuanhuai, a prestigious campaigner of the Westernization Movement, purchased the nearly derelict garden and had it refurbished and expanded to what it looks like today. Inheriting the devotion to rocks from Liu Rongfeng, Sheng Kang took it even further by collecting standing marble screens, ichthyolites

More than 700-Meter Long Covered Walkway

and Lingbi sacrificial rocks to strew around the garden. While diversifying the collection of precious rocks in the garden, Sheng made the garden one of the best in Jiangnan, and the nation. The quantity of rocks and their diversity makes the garden unrivalled in all of China.

The Lingering Garden is second only to the Humble Administrator's Garden in size among the gardens in Suzhou. It covers more than three hectares and is divided into four parts: the central, the eastern, the western and the northern part. Each part is connected to another by winding walkways that measure 700-plus meters in total.

The garden has all its scenery and buildings clustered in the central and eastern part, with the central part retaining most of the features from Liu Shu's time. An enormous pond in the center is its prime attraction. The western and northern parts feature artificial hills, and the eastern part is noted for the most diversified structural layout in Suzhou.

Lattice Window "Revealing" the Spring Scene

The entrance gate is located at the side gate of the original garden. In the middle of the gate hall there is a huge lacquer screen showing a panoramic view of the entire garden. All the pavilions, hills and flora are highlighted with gems of different colors.

Beyond the hallway, after walking through a long and winding path and across two tiny courtyards, you can see the central garden. Take your time to enjoy the two tiny and delicate courtyards that guard the spectacular view of the central garden. Across the courtyards the Green Shade Chamber can be found.

The chamber's open north side offers an ideal place to admire the scenery of the central pond. An old green maple tree more than 300 years old stands west of the chamber, the inspiration for the chamber's name. Though the tree is no longer the beauty it once was, it still has a regal bearing. The

Left: Shu Xiao Pavilion at the top of the Western Wild Mountain

Zigzag Bridge Covered with Wisteria as Viewed from The Green Shade Chamber

artificial hill nearby is The Virgin Hill, another name for girls of fair beauty, and one of the 12 hills installed by Liu Shu as part of his first collection.

Heading west across the Virgin Hill through the Green Shade Chamber, you will find the Ming Se Building that connects to the Han Bi Villa, both rooms part of one building. Ming Se, in Chinese, means brilliant and clear. To the south a small Tai Hu rockery leans against the wall, and the staircases leading upward are tucked away against the side of the cloud-shaped rockery.

The building, with windows on three sides for sightseeing, is shaped like a pleasure-boat. From across the pond, the boat seems to be on shimmering waters. The Han Bi Villa was the main structure built during Liu's time. It has 18 long windows on both the south and north sides. The southern courtyard has lake rocks piled high against walls and a flower terrace in the middle. To the north of the study is a terrace that overlooks the water. If you take your

Ming Se Building beside the Han Bi Villa

time, you can also see the pavilions shrouded by trees in the east, as well as mountainous peaks to the north-west. The hills and waters make the villa a perfect site to take in the breathtaking beauty of the central area.

To the west of the Han Bi Villa is the huge rockery that takes up the entire western and northern sides. Designed at first by Zhou Bingzhong, a hill-building master of the late Ming Dynasty, and built with yellow rocks, the hill had many Tai Hu rocks added during subsequent renovations. Despite its untraditional mixture of the two separate type of rocks, the hill still retains its splendor after hundreds of years. Three old gingko trees stand next to the southern part of the hill, facing the Ming Se Building across the pond. Several hundred years old, the gingko trees show off their lush leaves and enormous green canopy in the summer, their leaves turning bright yellow in the fall. Auspicious Cloud Peak, one of the top famous rocks in the garden, was later removed to the Textile Official Residence (No. 10 Secondary School of Suzhou today) in the Qing Dynasty, to greet Emperor Qianlong during his Jiangnan tour.

Han Bi Villa Facing the Middle Mountain Pond

Auspicious Cloud Peak in the East Garden

The Osmanthus Fragrance Pavilion Standing at the top of the Hill

To the west of the Han Bi Villa, a terrace climbs along the hill. These types of terraces are referred to as Hill-Climbing Terraces. Hiking upward along the terrace, you will reach the Osmanthus Fragrance Pavilion, located at the highest point of the central garden and surrounded by osmanthus trees. This Pavilion overlooks rolling hills and peaks that lead down to the Emerald Pond. The Small Fairy Islet in the middle of the pond has wisterias hanging over the winding bridge, making it look like the colored wings of phoenixes from a distance. The islet features a few pavilions tucked among the rocks and ancient trees.

From the Osmanthus Fragrance Pavilion, go across the creek via stone bridge to reach a tiny pavilion named "Ke Pavilion" at the northern hilltop. Ke Pavilion, in Chinese, is a homonym for "worth a pause", advice to the visitor to stay in the pavilion to take in the scenery. It has a particularly wonderful view of the Han Bi

Villa across the pond. The delicate Ke Pavilion on the hilltop gives a great contrast to the huge study near the water. The hexagonal stone table in the pavilion has a black surface with white stone lines, and gives out a low and solemn sound when knocked upon. This Lingbi stone table is very rare to see, especially its one meter diameter table surface.

From the northern side of the pavilion, a colored path winds along the hillside. Paved with colored pebbles and broken pieces of porcelain in the pattern of flowering crabapples, the path runs parallel with the walkway that zigzags along the garden wall. The walkway and the path finally join each other at the Distant Green Pavilion at the eastern corner of the central part.

A tiny two-storey building named the Distant Green Pavilion stands on a level area, flanked by rocks from North Mountain and Tai Hu. A green peony flower terrace built during the Ming Dynasty sits in the center with its east, west and north sides carved with delicate designs: two lions playing with a ball, a rhino staring at the moon and a horse galloping into the sky.

A colored path winding to the south leads to the Xiao Penglai Islet. Here, a creek from the north-west corner divides the hill into the western and the northern parts. Three charming small stone bridges cross over the creek. Xiao Penglai islet and the bridge that spans north to south, divides the pond into eastern and western parts.

With a wider area, the western part has countless trees in the north and several pavilions in the south, whereas the more secluded eastern part features

Above: Distant Green Pavilion **Right:** Ke Pavilion

a water courtyard with only two buildings — the Cool Breeze Pond House and the Hao Pu Pavilion, in two drastically different styles.

The Hao Pu Pavilion, facing waters on three sides, has two of Liu's original 12 peaks: the Yin Yue Peak on the southwest and the Kui Xiu Peak on the bank of Little East Bay. The name Yin Yue was inspired by the fact that the hole in the peak looks exactly like a full moon reflected in the water; the Kui Xiu Peak was named to remind the visitors of the Kui Mansion among the 28 constellations.

Looking north-east from the Hao Pu Pavilion across the water, Cool Breeze Pond House sits not far away. It forms the Chinese character Pin (品) along with the western building and Qu Xi Building to the south. This set of buildings, while offering beautiful sights of the surrounding scenery, separates the central and eastern parts of the garden. The Cool Breeze Pond House and Qu Xi Building, at the end of the northern and southern wings respectively, also work as connecting structures. Two open windows on the ground floor of Qu Xi Building reveal the scenery of the central part, while a group of lattice screens on the east leads to the southern courtyard of the Five-Peak Celestial House. The eastern wall of the ground floor is a windowless divider. Set in this wall are more than twenty Steles with famous calligraphic inscriptions, a rare treasure.

Small Fairy Islet leading to Wisteria-Covered Zigzag Bridges

The magnificent Five-Peak Celestial House is the main building of the eastern part, covering a total of 280 square meters. It is also known as the "No. 1 Hall in Jiangnan". The interior is divided into the southern and northern parts with a line of elegantly-carved lattice window and screens. Taking up three-quarters of the building, the bright

The Cold Breeze Pool Hall Facing a Small Pond

and spacious southern part was used for hosting parties. Installed in the middle of the room is a screen made of gingko wood. Twenty-four wall screens show delicate craftsmanship. To underscore the importance of rocks in the garden, stone was also used as decorations inside the halls: four marble screens hang on the left and right walls of the southern hall. The natural patterns on the marble slabs bears a resemblance to those in ink paintings. A standing round marble screen in the western side of the northern hall is an extraordinary piece, for it not only

Inside the Five-Peak Celestial Hall

One of the Three Treasures of the Lingering Garden — The Mounted Marble Screen

measures 1.4 meters in diameter but also presents a vivid likeness of a landscape painting, even hinting at a moon hidden behind the clouds on the upper left. Many say there are three treasures in the Lingering Garden: this very marble screen, the Cloud-Crowned Peak and its ichthyolite.

The Five-Peak Celestial House has a courtyard in the south, a building to its west and an enclosure in the east (where cranes were raised). The north-western corner of the hall joins a study named Ji Gu De Xiu Geng. On the joining eastern side of the complex is the Stone Forest Yard.

The magnificent rockery with rolling peaks in the south hall is a copy of Lu Mountain. These hills were more commonly used as the decoration for halls, and thus are referred to as "hall hills". This one is probably one of the biggest in Suzhou. The small northern courtyard is also adorned with a few

Looking out at the Small Stone Forest Courtyard

Monkey Peak

Inside the Bowing Peak Pavilion

lake rocks, forming an interesting contrast with the taller hill in the southern courtyard. Appearing like a sitting monkey, the peak at the front of the veranda is called the Monkey Peak, yet another one of Liu's 12 peaks.

The courtyard has a small structure in the middle with a brick table and stone stools which allow a moment of respite. Seven stylistically varying mini-gardens lie in each direction. Five rocks and two stalagmites collected by Liu Rongfeng are spread out on top of the steep Gan Xiao Peak. Standing four meters tall, Gan Xiao Peak is surrounded by banana trees, bamboo, and flowers, and resembles a three-dimensional painting from its various angles. Take a walk in the courtyard and enjoy the scenery both below and outside the windows.

Going east beyond the courtyard and along the winding walkway, you will catch sight of a garden named One Corner of East Garden, once the residence of its owner. It was ransacked by the Japanese soldiers during the Anti-Japanese War, and was later restored as a garden for displaying plants.

A stone gate on the northern face of the east garden faces a grand double-room hall called The Forest and Spring Hall, a construction built during

Left and Right: Inside the Forest and Spring Hall

Sheng's expansion efforts. This is one of the most magnificent buildings in the entire garden, featuring designs and beautiful patterns on the doors, windows, beams, and pillars. Four huge rosewood and marble screens hang on the eastern and western walls, framed with fascinating patterns.

The hall, along with the Cloud-Crowned Building in the north, Cloud-Crowned Platform in the west and the Cloud-Crowned Pavilion in the east, was built as a viewing complex to admire the three cloud-crowned peaks in the central courtyard.

Some call the peak "Guan-Yin" (a goddess in China's mythology) because it resembles the goddess wearing a cloak and standing on a turtle-like stone pedestal.

Among the three peaks, the Cloud-Crowned Peak is the biggest and therefore regarded as the most important one. The Cloud-Crowned Peak enjoys equal fame with Yu Ling Long at the Yu Garden in Shanghai and the Corrugated Cloud Peak at West Lake in Hangzhou. Sheng Kang acquired this rock during his later years, even purchasing land to place it. He had the pavilion expanded and dug a "Cloud-Washing Swamp" to counterbalance the huge peak. To enhance the grandeur of his favorite rock, Sheng had Xiu Yun and Rui Yun Peaks built on each side.

The Cloud-Crowned Peak, standing 6.5 meters high, is the tallest rockery in China.

Left: The Front Porch of the Forest and Spring Hall

"A Corner of the East Garden" — A Natural Stone Table in the Garden

Crowning-Cloud Peak Standing in front of the Cloud-Washing Swamp

Auspicious Cloud Peak on the Eastern Side of the Crowning-Cloud Peak

Cave Cloud Peak on the Western Side of the Crowning-Cloud Peak

Its delicate and twisty appearance has all the features required of a perfect Tai Hu Rock: "lean, wrinkled, hollowed, and perforated". Rising upward in a twisted manner, the Cloud-Crowned Peak has a huge hollow cave at the top. The two moderate sized peaks beside the Cloud-Crowned Peak have their own special features: Xiu Yun Peak has many little caves, whereas the Rui Yun Peak has a hollow and craggy look.

The Cloud-Washing Swamp in the south artfully reflects the silhouette of the peaks in the water. The southern tip of the pond joins the terrace of the Wood and Spring Hall. On the terrace, Tai Hu rocks are ingeniously positioned in the shape of an irregular arc to complement the Cloud-Crowned Peak in the north.

The two-storey Cloud-Crowned Building, on the opposite end of The Wood and Spring Hall, has four rosewood screens on the north wall framed with marble stones. Hidden in the stones is a four-character Chinese phrase, "Heavenly Garden where the Cloud Stops", a homage to the Cloud-Crowned Peak.

Crowning-Cloud Pavilion and The Crowning-Cloud Building behind the Pavilion

Crowning-Cloud Platform

Small Pond and Rockeries in the Miniature Landscape Garden

Three-Turn Zigzag Bridge and the Lively Water Pavilion in the Western Part of the Lingering Garden

The first floor of the building features a square block of stone embedded with fossils of fish. The most spectacular of them all is the 15-centimeter immature fish. This ichthyolite is one of the three treasures in the Lingering Garden.

Once we pass through the cave to the western section of the terrace we are in the northern part of the garden. Once dominated by beautiful countryside scenery, the northern part is now covered with giant bamboo and a few magnolia trees. The scenery behind the garden has been mostly destroyed.

Turn west on the gravel path that runs through the entire northern part to reach the western part of the garden. It features a huge earthen hill with maple and camphor trees. A stream from the south enhances the sensation of a natural forest.

The overall layout of the Lingering Garden tends to go from spectacular to plain. But throughout this varying layout, one thing that will make an everlasting impression is the collection of precious rocks.

The Garden of Cultivation

— A Legacy of Celebrated Ancient Scholars

Due to its special history, this Garden was virtually unknown before it was listed as a UN World Cultural Heritage site. Located in the north-west corner of Suzhou, the Garden of Cultivation espouses the aesthetical sentiments of the late Ming Dynasty and the early Qing Dynasty, a period known for high ambition.

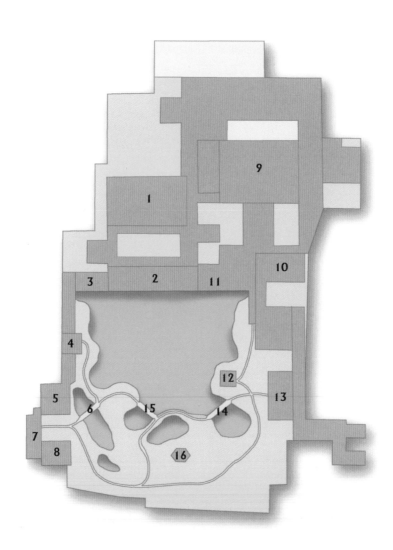

Plan of the Garden of Cultivation

1.博雅堂 [念祖堂] Bo Ya Tang [Nian Zu Tang] (Bo Ya Hall [The Ancestor-Commemorating Hall]) 2. 延光阁 Yan Guang Ge (Yan Guang Pavilion) 3. 思敬居 Si Jing Ju (The Remembering-the- Respectable Residence) 4. 响月廊 Xiang Yue Lang (Moon-Looking Corridor) 5. 香草居 Xiang Cao Ju (The Vanilla House) 6.浴鸥池Yu Ou Chi (Swimming Gull Pool) 7.鹤柴轩He Chai Xuan (The Crane Wood Chamber) 8. 南斋 Nan Zhai (The South Study) 9. 大厅 Da Ting (The Main Hall) 10. 世伦堂 Shi Lun Tang (The Secular Ethics Hall) 11. 谷书堂 Yang Gu Shu Tang (The Sunrise Study) 12. 乳鱼亭 Ru Yu Tang (Fish-Feeding Pavilion) 13. 思嗜轩 Si Shi Xuan (Hobby-Remembering Pavilion) 14. 乳鱼桥 Ru Yu Qiao (Fish-Feeding Bridge) 15. 度香桥 Du Xiang Qiao (The Measuring Fragrance Bridge) 16. 朝爽亭 Chao Shuang Ting (The Morning Cool Pavilion)

Transport:	Take the Tourists' Coach Line 1 and get off at the Jinmen Stop.
Admission:	RMB 3
Business Hours:	8 am-5 pm
Tips:	The Baby Fish Pavilion is the only example of Ming Dynasty architecture to have survived. Ancient colored drawings and floral designs remain intact on the roof beams of the Baby Fish Pavilion. Take some time to appreciate these precious rarities.

"A garden earns more fame with a better owner." Indeed, most of China's gardens have become famous because of their links to celebrated figures in history. Meanwhile, some were also undermined by their fame, for they were usually acquired by rich merchants with no taste for art, and no inclination to pursue the sequestered life of highly-cultivated intellectuals. The Garden of Cultivation, however, is an unusual gem because it remained

Main Gate of the Garden of Cultivation

unchanged despite its various owners. Therefore, even although it is small, the garden is part of the World Heritage list.

The Garden of Cultivation was possessed by three well-known scholars: Yuan Zugeng (1519-1590) of the Ming Dynasty who stepped down from his position in the government at the age of 40 to become a widely respected scholar; Wen Zhenmeng (1574-1638) who enjoyed a high reputation as the great-grandson of Wen Zhengming, a celebrated master painter in China's history, and served as the prime minister in the late Ming Dynasty; and Jiang Cai, a respected scholar and minister of Foreign Affairs during the late Ming Dynasty, who protested against corruption by exiling himself.

Brick Inscription on the Gate of the "Swimming Gull" Pond

After the Ming Dynasty collapsed, Jiang Cai refused to serve for the Qing Dynasty.

All three owners of the Garden of Cultivation were scholars known for their integrity. And this fact was the reason the Garden of Cultivation enjoyed such

View of the Garden of Cultivation

Ancient Wooden Pillar of the Bo Ya Hall, Characteristic of the Ming Dynasty Style

widespread fame in the early Qing Dynasty.

Afterwards, the garden fell into the hands of another owner and was converted into the office of a silk factory during the 19th year of Emperor Daoguang's rule in the Qing Dynasty (1839). In the early years of 20th century, the garden was severely damaged after a few of its rooms were used as ordinary residences. In 1979, the government started restoration of the Garden of Cultivation. With the help of historical illustrations of and literature about the garden, the garden was restored very close to its original appearance, both in layout and in style.

The Garden of Cultivation today covers just a bit more than 3,000 square meters, slightly smaller than its original size. Ponds are the central feature of this garden with a group of buildings in the north and rockeries and courtyards to the south.

Enter through the front gate. The Entrance Hall has three rooms. After turning three corners, you will arrive at the residential section in the northern part of the garden.

Go beyond the residential section of the garden, and you will see the "Bo Ya Hall", a main hall at the far southern end. The spacious Bo Ya Hall has five rooms, consisting of three halls and two living suites on the left and right. Take time to admire the woodwork in this structure. Most of it hails from the Ming Dynasty, and is rare and precious. The beams on the ceiling bear the carvings of mountains, fogs and clouds from the Ming Dynasty.

The old terrace that stretches to the water in front of the Bo Ya Hall was converted into a courtyard with winding terraces when it was used as the

Scenery Viewed though the windows of the Yan Guang Pavilion

office of the silk factory. The Yan Guang Pavilion, a big water pavilion, spans nearly half the pond, another addition to the south courtyard.

The Yan Guang Pavilion in the Garden of Cultivation is unusually big. With as many as five rooms, it joins the Yang Gu Shu Tang in the east and Si Jing Ju in the west to constitute one complex across the northern part of the garden.

As the biggest water pavilion in Suzhou, Yan Guang Pavilion has stone pillars and beams high above the water on its southern face that span most of the wide water surface. Originally, the pond had a size of more than 1,330 square meters. Having been narrowed considerably by the line of pavilions, the pond still has kept its grandeur, with coves in the south-east and south-west corners that make the pond seem to stretch on forever.

The Famous Expansive Pond of the Garden of Cultivation

The artificial hill in the south is mostly made up of earth, with the part facing the pond heaped with Tai Hu rocks forming a steep cliff all the way down to the water. Trees with enormous green canopies flourish on the rockery, giving an impression of a forest. According to historical records, the rockery had over 10 peaks during the early Qing Dynasty. Today, the rockery still retains much of its original style despite minor alterations.

The Sunrise Study, on the eastern side of the Yan Guang Pavilion, was named by Jiang. Yang Gu refers to the place where the sun rises, for the big study, facing west, would have been the site where the garden's owner gave his lectures. Today, it mostly faces south and the patio in the north-west corner draws natural light from the sun. On the eastern side, huge windows span all the way to the ground and a small terrace to the south leads to a room named the Lotus Chamber, also named by Jiang. The chamber used to

Fish-Feeding Pavilion and the Surrounding Rockery South of the Pond

Ming Dynasty Decorations on the Corner Roof Beams
of the Fish-Feeding Pavilion

be where the host took a break after giving lectures in the nearby study. The name "lotus" was inspired by *A Eulogy of Lotus*, a section from a great literary work by Zhou Dunyi of the Song Dynasty.

To the south of the Lotus Chamber a path leads to a small waterside pavilion with three sides facing the water. At first glance, the antique square pavilion seems to be same as the ones in other Suzhou gardens. However, it is one of the few legacies of the Ming Dynasty, the only surviving Ming construction in the entire Garden. Ancient painted patterns can still be found on the pillars and beams in the pavilion named "Ru Yu" — the word "Ru" meaning "feeding".

To the south of the pavilion is a cove in the south-east corner of the pond. Shrouded in a messy collection of rocks, the cove has a Rainbow Bridge constructed from six slabs of slate that form a slight arch.

Cross the bridge and you will reach the artificial hills south of the pond. Below the steep cliff, a winding path almost reaches the pond, following a precarious route to the bank until it splits into two when it reaches a huge rock. One path leads to the Du Xiang Qiao at the south-west corner of the pond and the other winds upward to the hilltop through a narrow cave. A hexagonal pavilion named Zhao Shuang sits on top of the hill and from there you can take in the mountains of southern Suzhou. Although the distant mountains are mostly blocked by high-rises nowadays, the pavilion still offers great sights of the Yan Guang Pavilion to the north of the pond. The pavilions seem to be floating above the shimmering water, presenting a breathtaking view.

A three-turn zigzag bridge named Du Xiang Qiao lies to the north-east at the foot of the hill. Almost touching the water, the low Du Xiang Qiao feels as if it is floating above the water. Across the bridge, a side courtyard known as Qin Lu can be accessed through a moon gate.

Measuring Fragrance Bridge Hovering Right Above the Water

Moon Gate Leading to the Celery Hut

Swimming-Gull Pool in the Courtyard of the Celery Hut

Of all the side courtyards in Suzhou gardens, Qin Lu courtyard is a highly unusual one because it features a pond instead of a rockery as its dominating feature. The pond with Tai Hu rock winds around the arched gate in the middle of the courtyard. A small stone bridge in front of the arch goes across the pond, to meet another bridge at its narrowest point. The Yu Ou Pond has its water flowing below the Du Xiang Bridge and then running out into a bigger pond. Small as the Yu Ou Pond is, it has two tiny bridges that create an interesting scenic contrast with the big pond outside the courtyard. Wen Zhenheng, the younger brother of the second garden owner Wen Zhenmeng wrote a monograph with instructions on how to build a pond. His philosophy is reflected in this very small pond, a wonderful sample of the style of the Ming Dynasty. To its south a rock flower terrace sits low on the ground. Behind it bamboo thrives, giving the courtyard an elegant look. To the west of the courtyard there is a building complex shaped like the Chinese character Pin (品), with the Vanilla House to the north and the South Study to the south. A small area between them has a rock flower terrace in the middle and a gate leading out into the courtyard. The room that projects out from the hall's west side is called the Crane Wood Chamber since the site used to be an enclosure for raising cranes during Jiang's time.

To the north of the Vanilla House, a walkway named Moon-Looking Corridor runs along the wall from north to south. Originally named by Jiang, Xiang Yue also appears in the eulogistic poems of Wang Shizhen who depicted it as a delicate corridor winding along shady trees. Today, it is a straight path. The word "Xiang" is a homonym of another word meaning "to". Therefore, the name "Xiang Yue" implies an aspiration to the moon. To its east, diagonally opposite, is the old Yang Gu Shu Tang. Yang Gu refers to the shelter from the rising sun, while Xiang Yue means

Open Window of the Moon-Looking Corridor

that the moon is hidden. In Chinese, The characters "Sun" and "Moon" can combine to mean "Ming". Perhaps the names of these two buildings express a faint hope on the part of its the owner that the Ming Dynasty will return once again, just like a temporarily invisible sun and moon. The owner probably used homonyms for the names in order to ward off the suspicions of Qing officials.

Epilogue

I have lived in Suzhou for 20 years, and the gardens have given me shelter from all my troubles; I have derived great joy from visiting the gardens during inclement weather when few tourists dare to go out. After staring at a stone or a tree for a long time, I felt a vital connection with it. As a result, I thought it could not be difficult to scribble down every detail about these gardens. However, I was frustrated to find that the writing process was unexpectedly slow as I was caught between trying to explore the profound cultural significance of the gardens, and presenting their visual details. I was also torn between distinguishing them from one another, while summing up the common points in their overall designs. The result was that I spent much more time deciding what to delete than what to write. Even so, I was not completely satisfied with the content.

A similar example of such conflict can also be found in the classical gardens of Suzhou, for they were at first constructed as a sequestered landscape offering an outlet for spiritually cultivated scholars, but were then purchased by officials and rich merchants who posed as lovers of culture. These owners had luxury touches added to the gardens and made some areas look like polished antiques, undermining their original simplicity.

I would like to extend my acknowledgement to Zhu Shiwei, the general manager of Suzhou Sansi Technology Company who took many wonderful photographs, Huang Ruoyu from the Central Academy of Fine Arts who drew plans for each garden, and Wang Lixiang and Zheng Mingbao from the Shanghai Classic Publishing House who offered valuable advice on the book. Without them, I could not have come this far.

I do hope that the book can be of some assistance to readers who want to visit or have already toured Suzhou's gardens, and help them have a better understanding of these great artistic works.

Xia Dynasty	c.2100B.C.- c.1600B.C.
Shang Dynasty	c.1600B.C.- c.1100B.C.
Zhou Dynasty	c.1100B.C.- c.221B.C.
Western Zhou Dynasty	c.1027B.C.- c.771B.C.
Eastern Zhou Dynasty	770B.C.- 256B.C.
Spring and Autumn Period	770B.C.- 476B.C.
Warring States Period	476B.C.- 256B.C.
Qin Dynasty	221B.C.- 206B.C.
Han Dynasty	206B.C.- 220A.D.
Western Han Dynasty	206B.C.- 25A.D.
Eastern Han Dynasty	25A.D.- 220A.D.
Three Kingdoms	220A.D.- 280A.D.
Wei	220A.D.- 265A.D.
Shu Han	221A.D.- 263A.D.
Wu	222A.D.- 280A.D.
Jin Dynasty	265A.D.- 420A.D.
Western Jin	265A.D.- 317A.D.
Eastern Jin	317A.D.- 420A.D.
Northern and Southern Dynasties	420A.D.- 589A.D.
Southern Dynasties (Song, Qi, Liang, Chen)	420A.D.- 589A.D.
Norther Dynasty	439A.D.- 581A.D.
Sui Dynasty	581A.D.- 618A.D.
Tang Dynasty	618A.D.- 907A.D.
Five Dynasties	907A.D.- 960A.D.
Song Dynasty	960A.D.- 1279A.D.
Northern Song	960A.D.- 1127A.D.
Southern Song	1127A.D.- 1279A.D.
Yuan Dynasty	1279A.D.- 1368A.D.
Ming Dynasty	1368A.D.- 1644A.D.
Qing Dynasty	1644A.D.- 1911A.D.